35

DAYS OF CONFIDENCE

Find Your Voice,
Fulfill Your Dreams
and Focus Your Inner Power

ALYSSA A. AUSTIN

ISBN: 978-0-578-43832-0

DOWNLOAD THE 35 DAYS OF CONFIDENCE WORKBOOK FREE!

READ THIS FIRST

Just to say thanks for buying my book, I would like to give you the accompanying workbook 100% FREE!

As you'll see, this book is FULL of action exercises. If you purchased the physical version, you can certainly write your answers in the margins, but if you'd prefer to keep them clean (or if you purchased the Kindle version), download the free 35 Days of Confidence Workbook, which contains each day's Challenge activity. You can download it as many times as you'd like!

TO DOWNLOAD GO TO:
poisedandprofessional.com/free-workbook

Dedication

I would like to dedicate this book to:

My Parents
My mom and dad – I will never be able to say thank you enough for raising me to be confident, strong, and ready to take on the world. Mom - not everyone is fortunate to grow up with a mother who is encouraging and supportive. Even fewer people are fortunate enough to grow up with a mother who truly believes in them and thinks their child can do anything – literally anything. Thank you, mom and dad, for fostering that belief. "Because you believed in me, I believed in me."

My Brothers
Nick, Hunter, and Noah – you inspire and motivate me more than you know. Thank you for being supportive and willing to offer advice throughout this process.

My Husband
Mike – without you, none of this would have been possible, and I am so, so grateful for your love and support. Thank you for believing in me, and always pushing me to be the best version of myself. I love you.

My Colleagues
To my mentor, Brian Tracy, who helped to inspire my fascination with personal development, and kickstart the belief in myself that I was meant for something bigger.

To my coworkers and colleagues, specifically those at Brandetize, for helping me learn and grow in this space, and equipping me with the tools to pursue this dream.

To everyone I've ever shared the stage with – for allowing me to do what I love and grow exponentially in the process. So much of what I teach is because of what I learned from you.

Table of Contents

Introduction

There are few things in this world that you can NEVER have enough of.

Love, friendship, good wine, laughter...

And confidence.

I'm going to reveal something to you right now: *Confidence is the key to ALL success in life.*

Regardless of what you want to do, who you want to become, and what your hopes and dreams are, confidence WILL help you achieve it. Because true confidence comes from knowing exactly who you are, and what you want in life, and then fiercely pursuing it.

You're probably heard the phrase, "Whether you think you can, or you think you can't, you're right". The key word here is "think".

Everything we do, everything we feel, everything we think starts in the same place: **our mind.** And this is where confidence is created and nurtured as well: within our minds. The mind is the origin point of confidence.

And here's another secret:

*You have every reason in the world to be completely, 100% confident in who you are **at this very moment.***

If you believe that already – great! This book will serve as an excellent exercise in affirmation for you.

And if you don't – don't worry. We will get you there. It's all a matter of learning. Like riding a bike or teaching yourself a new language, confidence is a learned skill.

You see, I have been fascinated by the science of human communication and connection for years. I've put in hundreds of hours of study on the topics of communication, performance, productivity, leadership, ambition, and more. I am a voracious consumer of information, and pride myself on being pretty darn good at sharing that information with others in an easily understood and memorable way. My specialty, as a friend of mine once beautifully articulated, is "creating clarity from chaos".

But I'm NO EXPERT. I can't state that enough. I'm a person, just like you, who's doing their best to live a happy, fulfilled, confident life.

However, I do have a secret skill that I have come to realize it is my duty to share... I have **killer confidence**. And I can attribute my confidence to three key aspects of my life: my upbringing, my life as a performer, and my work as a communications professional.

I was fortunate enough to grow up with incredible love and support from my family, specifically my mom. From the day I was born, she has been my number one fan and life advocate. And I am convinced that is 100% because of her and the way she raised me that I have even an iota of the confidence I have as an adult. My mom raised me with the undying, unwavering belief and affirmation that I could do anything I could put my mind to. She told me enough times in my child and young adult life that it became very easy to believe: **I can do anything.** If I put my mind to it, and I really try (that's the key – there has to be effort), I can do anything.

It was in a large part due to my mom that I achieved my second confidence aspect: performing. I started dancing at a very young age, which forced me to become very comfortable in the spotlight (and even learn to love it!) Years later, as a performer, I've sang, danced, and acted on stage, gone on hundreds of auditions, completed thousands of performances for audiences small and large (up to 106,000 people, actually!)

And finally, as a communications professional, I've given hundreds of business presentations and had to speak to groups of colleagues much more "senior" than myself. I've even participated in public speaking competitions. I've also worked one-on-one with coworkers and direct reports to help them craft their ideal professional path, and improve their confidence along the way.

I began this book not as a book at all, but as a personal exercise to help me document the practices that help *me* feel my most confident self. Similar to reading a self-help book, I had found that writing out my own "self-help" was cathartic and action-driving on its own. So, I kept writing, and writing and well... here we are.

My goal for you in reading this book is to become **truly confident and happy in who you are right NOW, and arm you with the tools you need to obtain everything you want out of life (and then some).**

Over the course of this book, we're going to go through the five core pillars that provide the foundations for a confident life. I've created and lead hundreds of action exercises around the topic of confidence, and these five pillars are the foundational elements that I keep coming back to again and again.

They are:

1. Self-Discovery
2. Positive Mental Attitude

3. Self-Improvement
4. The Physical Body
5. Taking Action

These pillars are ordered in such a way that we will build on them, day-by-day, week-by-week, from the inside out—all with the goal of helping you not only increase your self-confidence, but make it a habit in your daily life.

By the end of these 35 days, confidence will just be "something that you do". You will be armed with daily rituals and practices to keep it at the forefront of your personality and every day actions. Some of the chapters are short, and some of the chapters are long, but the end goal is the same: to help you find your voice, fulfill your dreams and focus your inner power, so that you can create your **most confident, authentic, ideal life.**

And the great thing about these lessons and exercises is that they are timeless. Sure, you'll start your #35DaysofConfidence journey today, but in three months, six months, a year... if you're feeling as though you need a confidence boost? You can start the challenge all over again.

I hope you stick around until Day 35—because I promise, **there is something here for you.** There is something potentially world-shaking for you to discover about yourself and the life you've always imagined and dreamed up for yourself between now and the end of this book.

Best case scenario? Your life changes completely and positively as a result of reading this book and going through the accompanying exercises. Worst case scenario? You learn a couple new things. Either way, isn't it worth a shot?

I encourage you to invest in a journal that you can use alongside your journey for the next 35 days—I'm going to be asking you to really dig deep inside yourself and dream, and there's no better (and more action-inspiring) way to do that than on paper.

Starting now, I'm going to show you just how confidence can change your life… if you're willing to change yourself.

Let's get started.

Week 1: Self-Discovery

The first step of the journey to supreme self-confidence has to do with developing an in-depth understanding of
who you are.

Think of it this way: if your friend asked you for a dinner recommendation, you wouldn't vouch for a restaurant you'd never been to before, would you? No—you'd give her the name of a spot you know and love. Where the menu is expansive, the ambiance is comforting, and the prices are decent. A place you'd feel confident would meet and exceed her expectations.

In order to be truly confident, you must do the same thing for yourself. You must understand who you are, what you want, and what makes you unique. There are many definitions of self-confidence, but the one that I keep coming back to again and again, and the one that has rang true through all my hours of study is this: **true confidence comes from knowing exactly who you are and what you want.**

We'll explore these concepts through seven days of self-discovery, starting... now!

1

Believe in Yourself

"She believed she could, so she did."

We start our #35DaysofConfidence with the core lesson of this book.

Above all else: **believe in yourself.** You are your own biggest cheerleader. You *have* to be!

Because your confidence levels and the way you feel about yourself is entirely up to you. It's not up to your mom, your dad, your spouse, your significant other, your best friends, your worst enemies, your coworkers, your castmates, your boss, your director, or ANYONE else!

Remember: It's nice, but not necessary to receive external validation.

Which means that you (and no one else) are responsible for becoming your biggest cheerleader. It's helpful to have others in your corner, but nothing will skyrocket your confidence or self-worth more than believing that you, yourself, are truly awesome.

Believing in yourself is one of the best things, if not THE best thing, you can do for yourself.

This is the core goal of this challenge, and we will build on it for the next 34 days.

Here is your Day 1 Challenge:

*Think back to one time when you believed in yourself fully and completely in your ability to achieve a goal, complete a task, or answer a call. **What did it feel like?** Why were you so confident? How can you create more of that feeling in the future?*

2

Identity

"This above all: to thine own self be true."
-William Shakespeare

One of the best places to start on your journey to supreme self-confidence is by **getting to know yourself,** inside-and-out. Sure, we all *to some extent* know ourselves. We know what we look like (whether we're okay with it or not), we know what we like and dislike, we know where we live, what we do for work and so on and so forth. But that's all just really surface-level stuff, isn't it?

An essential step on the journey to becoming 100% confident in yourself is 100% understanding who you are.

The more you know about yourself, the more you can work on strengthening your strengths, understanding and improving your weaknesses, and developing what it is about you that makes you truly unique!

Because you ARE unique. No one in the world is quite like you. Dr. Seuss expressed it best in his quintessential Dr. Seuss way:

"Today you are you, that is truer than true. There is no one alive who is youer than you."

And your differences are what make you **special.**

I can say this first-hand from working in the performance industry, where standing out is a GOOD thing. You must embrace the things that make you unique, whether it's your hair color, your singing voice, your fashion sense, your "quirks," or ANYTHING else. These are the things that make you special. That make you *memorable.*

And I realize this can be hard to do. Especially when we go through the formative stages of our lives—middle school, high school, college... maybe even entering a new place of work. In those stages, all we want to do is fit in. All we want to do is be like everyone else.

But being just like everyone else will never earn you recognition for YOUR awesomeness.

Don't waste your time trying to be just like someone else. Because that person already exists. Create your own legacy!

So, take a moment and think—What are YOU good at? Better than everyone else at, actually! What do you like about yourself? What makes you unique?

Knowing who you are, being able to identify your strengths, your weaknesses, what make YOU you... and then being okay with all of that, is a milestone on the road to self-confidence. It's in our imperfections, and our uniqueness, where we find out who we truly are!

Here is your Day 2 Challenge:

*Take 2 minutes and write down **10 things that make YOU unique.** They can be big or small, self-defining or trivial. The only important thing is that you write 10 things that make you YOU.*

3

Realization

"The first step to getting what you want out of life is this: Decide what you want."

Perhaps one of the most powerful things we can do on our journey to supreme self-confidence, and living our ideal life is realizing and NAMING exactly what it is that we want.

Think of it this way: if you can't say **what it is that you want,** how can you expect to achieve it?

You could have the most finely tuned, expensive, state-of-the-art compass in all the land, but unless you have a destination, your journey will be unsuccessful.

So, start now. What do you want? *Really.* Not what you *think* you should want, not what your family thinks you should want, not what the generic standards of "society" say you should want. YOU. If you could wave a magic wand, and have your ideal life materialize in front of your very eyes, what would it look like? Here are some questions to get you started:

How do you want to make a living? Would you be an entrepreneur who works from the comfort of her own computer and travels the world? Would you have an upper-management role at your current place of employment? Maybe work at a totally different place of employment from where you are now? Would you be working at ALL? Would you spend your days making people's lives better? Teaching people? Healing people? Performing? Selling products that make a difference? What is your DREAM job?

Where would you live? Would you live in your current city, or somewhere across the country, or even across the world? Would you live in a posh New York City apartment? A cottage on the beach in Florida? A mansion on the cliffs of Newport, Rhode Island? Maybe you are a total nomad who travels from place to place letting the universe create your path? Where is your ideal place of residence?

Who would you live with? Would you live with a significant other whom you currently have? A significant other whom you have yet to meet? Your family? Your children? If you don't have children, do you want children? Do you want to live totally and 100% alone? That's cool too. Who do you want to spend time with?

How would you spend your time? Aside from the time you spent creating your "living" (if that's your path), how do you want to occupy your days? Going to school or studying to improve yourself in your chosen field? Reading in the comfort of a cozy armchair in your own home? Traveling to exotic destinations all over the world? Surfing at the beach? Meditating on a grassy hillside? Working out? Hanging out with friends? Cherishing time with your family?

The choice of how you live your life is YOURS.

It really is.

You just have to decide what exactly it is that you want.

Realize it. Name it. Claim it as your own. And now, let's start creating it!

Here is your Day 3 Challenge:

If a genie appeared in front of you right now, and said you had three wishes to create your perfect life, what would you ask for? Use the questions above to write 3-5 sentences describing your ideal life. We're going to call this your **Aspiration Statement.** *When you finish writing these sentences, finish your paragraph with: "This is what I want. And I will achieve it".*

Want an example? Here's mine:

I want to make a living helping other women become the most confident, best versions of themselves, so they feel as though they can take on the world, because the world NEEDS more confident women. I want to create my living in this way, so I have freedom over my own schedule to dedicate time to my family and my passion of performing. I want to be able to travel, spend time with my family, and cultivate a home life that gives me peace and fulfillment. I want to live in San Diego with my husband and my dog, and move overseas or to another state in the next 3 years.

This is what I want. And I will achieve it.

Keep this paragraph close by. Or better yet, hang it in a place of prominence in your daily life. We will be coming back to it often!

4

Goal-Setting

"A dream without a plan is just a wish."

What are your goals in life? What do you want to achieve?

For some of you, the answer to those questions might be easy, and top of mind.

For others, you may *really* have to think about your goals... and you wouldn't be alone!

Numerous studies have shown that less than 3% of Americans have set goals, and less than 1% review and rewrite their goals on a daily basis.

Let that sink in: **less than 1% of people** in the United States have ever written down the things they want to achieve most in this world...

That's crazy!

And when we look at that 1%, what we find is pretty amazing. The people who not only write down and document their goals, but also rewrite them and revisit them consistently, are at least 10 times more successful than their non-goal-writing counterparts.

So why is goal-setting so important? Yes, it will help you become more successful, but *why* is that?

This is because: If you create the habit of being able to set goals and achieve them regularly, you will have **unlocked the key to success.**

If you think about it in the simplest terms, all achievement in the world comes down to setting goals and then achieving those goals. Every big goal can be broken down into a sequence of smaller, more achievable goals, in the same way that any huge task can be broken down into smaller, more achievable tasks. From there it's just a matter of time and continued effort until each goal is achieved.

So, if you want to achieve your goals, if you really want to turn your thoughts, your dreams into action, the best place to start is by **writing them down.**

These goals can be big or small. They can be things that you want to accomplish today, this week, the month, this year... even in the next 10 years or at some point in your life!

And truth be told—you should have goals for ALL these time intervals. Starting with your lifetime goals, you can break down the action steps, then map them to years, months and even days. But we'll cover this in detail in Week 5: "Taking Action".

That being said, you can probably guess what today's challenge is going to be...

Here is your Day 4 Challenge:

Based on your realization statement from yesterday, **craft three goals for this year.**

A great guideline to follow here is to create: one relationship-based goal, one financial or achievement-based goal, and one health-based goal.

These can be long term (several months) or short term (this month) goals, but they should all be goals you want to achieve this calendar year.

Write them down right now.

And then tomorrow when you wake up and you are making your plans for the day, write them down again. There's only three of them, so this shouldn't take you longer than 60 seconds.

5

Responsibility

"For the way you act, the way you feel, and the way you live: You are responsible."

Here's a saying that you've probably seen or heard before at some point in your life: *"If you don't like something, change it. If you can't change it, change your attitude."*

I love this quote so much because of its simplicity—whether we can or can't control something, our response and our actions are still OURS to take.

We are responsible.

At any moment in time, you are responsible for **the words that come out of your mouth.** Whether they are positive or negative, encouraging or discouraging, helpful or hurtful.

At any moment in time, you are responsible **for the actions you take.** You are responsible for how you spend your time, the people you spend your time with, and how you treat yourself and others. You may not be responsible for the problems you encounter, but you are fully responsible for your reactions.

You are responsible for your priorities.

You are responsible for the thoughts that live in your head.

You are responsible for *your own life.*

There's a saying in theatre that I learned when I was very young: "acting is reacting". Meaning, that in its truest, most basic form, "acting" is reacting to the world and the people around you. And you are responsible for your "acting".

The idea that you are responsible for your own actions, your own feelings, the direction of your own life is not dependent on whether or not you believe in a higher power, the idea of fate, or any other guiding force in this world. They both exist simultaneously.

It's SO easy to make excuses. How many times have you either heard or vocalized one of these lines – or something similar?

"I wanted to go to the gym today, but I ran out of time."
"I wanted to take that vacation this year, but work got too busy."
"I wanted to save a certain amount of money this year, but I had too many bills to pay off."
"I wanted to get married, but I guess I'm just not good/pretty/worthy enough."

There's a great moment from the movie, "The Holiday," that explains the idea of taking responsibility for your own life in a way that has always stuck with me.

Kate Winslet's character, Iris, is down in the dumps, as it seems everything has just gone wrong for her, and she can't seem to dig herself out of this hole. Arthur, her delightful, older neighbor tells her:

"In the movies, we have leading ladies and we have the best friend. I can tell that you're a leading lady but you're acting like the best friend..."

To which she responds: *"You're right; you're supposed to be the leading lady in your own life, for God's sake."*

Choose to be Kate Winslet today (and every day). Take responsibility and become the leading lady of your own life!

Here is your Day 5 Challenge:

The sooner you accept and internalize the notion that you (and only you) are responsible for your own life, the better. **Say out loud to yourself, right now: "I am responsible."**

Repeat this phrase throughout the rest of your day—when you're confronted with a challenge, when you need to do something you don't quite feel like doing... Heck, you can even use it as a motivational tool! The important thing is to repeat it out loud, and to repeat it often.

I turn this phrase into a mantra that I use to start my days: "I am responsible for my actions and my thoughts today. It's going to be a great day!"

Give this a try when you wake up tomorrow.

6

Motivation

"Motivation is what gets you started.
Habit is what keeps you going."
-Jim Ryun

The quote above is from Jim Ryun, a former American politician and track and field athlete. I love it because not only does it articulate the role of today's topic, motivation, in driving your journey towards your ideal life, it also reveals the role of habit in keeping the journey moving. And creating habits is what this challenge is all about!

Motivation is an interesting concept.

If you Google "motivation" right now, you'll be met with over 1 billion search results(!) There's certainly no lack of "motivation" available to us, but unfortunately motivation is not found that easily. At least not *really.*

What motivates one person can be totally meaningless to someone else. Motivation is subjective. It is internal. It is **uniquely individual** in nature.

And yet it is VITAL to success!

Think back to the last championship sports game you watched, the last awards acceptance speech—it's pretty routine that at some point in the recipient's spiel, they thank the people who contributed to their success, the people who kept them going. They thank their motivators.

I have found that motivation really sticks, really persists when it's tied to **relationships.** Because relationships really are what drive us as human beings. We long for community and inclusion. We want to be loved. Our relationships fuel us and keep us going, even when not much else can.

Here's a great example: say you have two people whose goal is to lose 10 pounds. One wants to lose the weight to look better in a bathing suit. The other wants to lose weight to become healthier, keep sickness at bay, and live a long and happy life with her family and loved ones.

Who do you think will ultimately be successful? Maybe (hopefully!) both of them, but you can bet that the second person, whose motivations are tied to relationships, will be more persistent in their journey.

This brings me to another point: As important as it is to find the things (and the people) that motivate you, it is equally important to identify the things (and the people) that do not.

When it comes to relationships, whether we realize it or not, we are greatly influenced by those closest to us. They affect our way of thinking, our self-esteem, and our decisions. There's a popular school of thought (originally from Jim Rohn) that you are the average of the five people who you spend the most time with. If those people are anything less than supportive, uplifting, inspiring—people who generally make you BETTER—then you need to make some personnel changes.

Here's a final quote to end today's lesson on motivation:

"Wanting something is not enough. You must hunger for it. Your motivation must be absolutely compelling in order to overcome the obstacles that will invariably come your way." -Les Brown

Here is your Day 6 Challenge:

Pull out your handy-dandy journal and answer the following questions:

1) What or who motivates you?
2) What gives you strength? (When do you feel strongest?)
3) What weakens you? (When do you feel most unsure, unconfident, unhappy?)

Once you complete these questions, take an additional 2 minutes to think how you can amplify what strengthens you in your daily life, and diminish what weakens you.

Circle 2 strength elements *that you're going to focus on experiencing MORE of in the next week.*

Strike out 2 weakness elements *that you're going to focus on experiencing LESS of in the next week.*

7

Mindset

"Whether you think you can, or you think you can't, you're right."
-Henry Ford

<hr/>

Picture this: you're waiting for the elevator on your way up to work. You're staring at the mirrored doors thinking, "Man, I really don't like my outfit today. What was I thinking when I got dressed?"

As you're staring down your reflection and questionable outfit choice in the mirror, a fellow woman approaches the elevator.

"LOVE that top!" she exclaims. "Where did you get it?"

You say "thank you," do the required sharing of purchase details, and think to yourself, "Hey, maybe this top is actually pretty awesome!" And you exit the elevator with some renewed pep in your step.

All because someone gave you some assurance.

The brain is funny that way. If you tell yourself something enough times, or if you are told something enough times, you will eventually believe it to be true. (Unfortunately, this works with negative talk just as well as it does with positive talk... but we'll talk about that in a little while). The good news is, it's just as easy to believe you're awesome, capable, confident, deserving, AMAZING as it is to believe you're not. It's all a matter of what you choose to believe.

Bottom line: What we tell repeatedly ourselves is what we will inevitably think.

This is why **affirmations** are such a powerful tool for change.

Affirmations are phrases or sentences aimed to affect the conscious and the subconscious mind.

Through vocalization, affirmations bring up related mental images into the mind, that inspire, energize and motivate... and fulfill any number of desired purposes, both automatically and involuntarily.

And, affirmations can be ANYTHING you want them to be! Here are some of my favorites:

I am bright, brilliant and beautiful.

I am beautiful, strong, and capable.

I can do anything I put my mind to.

I deserve this.

Good things happen to me every day.

Go ahead and repeat one of those out loud right now. Repeating affirmations and repeatedly being exposed to the resulting mental images affect the subconscious mind, which in turn influences behavior, habits, actions, and reactions, and helps create positive, lasting transformation.

Affirmations often receive a bad rap for being kind of fluffy and "woo-woo", but you can't deny their effectiveness. Which is why we're going to use them in today's challenge, and our final challenge of Week 1!

Here is your Day 7 Challenge:

*We're going to talk about "power phrases" for today's challenge. When I say "power phrase," I mean a **short, three-word phrase** that you can anchor on and repeat to yourself both throughout the day and in times of stress and nervousness.*

I find that adjectives work best: adjectives that describe you in your ideal state. The person you want to be, and the person you are more than capable of becoming!

Take a look back at your Day 3 Realization (your Aspiration Statement) and your Day 4 Goals—Are there specific attributes that you need to develop to accomplish those goals? What character traits will serve you along the way to your journey?

*Find three words that work for you. Or at least three to start with to create your first power phrase. It can change over time if it's not working for you, or you can have more than one for various scenarios and needs. The important thing is to **start.***

Write down your power phrase—in your journal, on a note in your phone, on a post-it note at your desk—and commit it to memory.

Now the fun part—find a place in your daily routine where you can practice saying your power phrase out loud to yourself. A great suggestion a friend of mine shared was every time you use the restroom—after you finishing washing your hands, say your power phrase out loud in front of the mirror. If you're in a public bathroom, maybe check for strangers first.... (Or don't! OWN IT!)

Saying these words out loud gives them power. Saying these words out loud gives YOU power. Try it for a week, and see how you feel. I promise you won't be disappointed.

Week 2: Positive Mental Attitude

Welcome to Week 2, A.K.A., "sunshine and rainbows week!" (Just kidding... kind of...) This week we're talking about all thing related to developing and keeping a

Positive Mental Attitude.

Before we begin, I want to clarify the fact that positivity is a state of mind. I once had the honor of listening a speaker who drove home the idea of positive outlook as a choice: "Each day when you wake up, you have the choice to decide whether today is going to be a good day or a bad day." It's 100% up to you. Your outlook determines your reactions, which determine your mood.

Positivity is a choice.

Over the next seven days, we're going to dive deep into the role of positivity (and all things that influence positivity) on the journey to supreme self-confidence. We'll also go through seven different challenges and action exercises for making positivity a habit.

Let's do this!

8

Happiness

"Whatever makes you happy, just do that."

I have this special coffee mug I like to use in the mornings. It's black and white-striped with, "Whatever makes you sparkle, just do that," written in cursive gold lettering on the sides.

Even on my darkest, most self-doubt-ridden, negativity-filled mornings, this coffee cup makes me happy. Because that cutesy truism that's printed on the side is a reminder for me that I am on the right path for myself. That by pursuing, "what makes me sparkle," I am working on living my best life.

And here's why: **If you focus on spending your time doing the things that you love, you will spend more time being happier, most positive and more confident.**

Maybe you just read through that last sentence and thought, "Okay, happier? Sure. More positive? Makes sense... But more confident? How does that one play into doing the things that you love?"

The answer is simple: it all has to do with **fulfillment.**

Let's use an example here to explain what I mean. Let's imagine for a moment that you're a rocket scientist (go you!) Now, you could be the most skilled, most successful, most highly-paid rocket scientist in the world... but if you hate what you're doing every day, you're never going to feel fulfilled by your work. If you don't feel fulfilled, you'll also never feel 100% confident that you're doing what you're meant to be doing in this world, and you're never going to find and live your *best* life.

When we do things that make us unhappy (whether intentionally or unintentionally), it becomes very hard to maintain our confidence in ourselves.

I'm going to reveal something here that really changed my life, ready? Here goes:

Happiness is the KEY to confidence.

Doing the things that make you happy will fuel you soul, and give you fulfillment, joy and confidence.

It's that simple.

Here is your Day 8 Challenge:

Getting clear about what makes you happy and makes you feel the most like the most kickass version of yourself will advance you leaps and bounds on the path towards becoming your most confident self.

Take five minutes now and create a "things that make me happy" list. What do you enjoy doing? Seeing? Reading? Write it ALL down.

The next step is a bit harder. Take a look at your current day, whether it be your planner, your to-do list, your calendar, or just thinking ahead to what you have going on, and evaluate: **Are any of the things I just wrote down on my happiness list on my to-do list today?**

If not, figure out a way to fit one of them in... right now! It may sound trite, but life is too short to NOT make time for the things that make you happy.

9

Gratitude

*"Learn to be thankful for what you already have,
while you pursue all that you want."*
-Jim Rohn

In my years of study of human behavior and the attainability of self-confidence, I have found that there's one core value that confidence always comes back to: and that's **gratitude.**

Feelings of gratitude and feelings of confidence are directly related.

This is because the more grateful you are for all that you have, the more you realize ALL that you have to be grateful for... and more and more awesome things begin to become apparent in your life. It's a self-perpetuating relationship. And once you begin to reframe your mindset for constant gratitude, you will continually gain MORE things to be grateful for.

The truth is, everyone has countless reasons to be thankful. But sometimes it doesn't feel that way. Maybe you're having a bad day, a bad week, heck, even a bad year.

But regardless of any of that, there is always, always, **always** something to be grateful for.

So, start with the basics: You are alive. You are healthy. You have a roof over your head. You had enough money to buy this book (or a kind friend who lent it to you). Start general and whittle down into the more specific reasons you have to be grateful.

Develop the habit of going through this exercise first thing in the morning as you start each day. Before you get out of bed each morning, make a mental list of at least three things you are grateful for. It's a brilliant way to start the day because it immediately frames your mind positively, and helps set you up for a great day ahead!

Being grateful is all a matter of perspective. Choose gratitude for what you have, not longing for the things you don't (which we'll talk more about later.)

Here is your Day 9 Challenge:

Here's how to begin making gratitude a habit in your daily life, and how to start building your confidence as a result.

The first step to gratitude is awareness. Making an active choice to be grateful opens your eyes to all the wonderful stuff you currently have going on in your life. In fact, take a moment right now and grab a pen and a piece of paper (if your computer or some other digital device happens to be closer, then that's fine too, but I strongly recommend pen and paper... you'll see why in a moment). Write down everything that you are grateful for today. These things can be general ("I'm grateful for my family"), or incredibly specific ("The awesome Pilates workout I did this morning"). They can be deep reflections ("I'm grateful for a spouse who loves and supports *me"), or more trivial ("I'm grateful for how kickass my butt looks in these new jeans"). It doesn't matter! The point is to write down as many things as possible that you are grateful for right now.*

Once you finish your list – I find the stopping point comes pretty naturally – it's really hard not to sit back and go, "Wow... I have a lot to be grateful for." And sometimes just that is enough to dial up your gratitude meter and set your course for an awesome day.

*A great way to take your gratitude practice to the next level is by starting (and committing to) a **Gratitude Journal.** I find that, by creating a journal, gratitude takes on a physical manifestation: This is my gratitude journal. This is where I write down everything that I'm grateful for. This journal is a manifestation of all the good in my life.*

Plus... it's freaking fun. My Gratitude Journal right now is a beautiful purple hardbound book with an elephant on the front that a very thoughtful colleague brought back for me after his trip to Thailand. I was grateful (and touched) that he thought to bring me back a gift, so it seemed a fitting repository for my daily gratitude lists.

My best days tend to happen when I start the morning with just 2-3 minutes (that's all it takes!) of writing in my Gratitude Journal. And that's not a coincidence. Gratitude frames your mind for a positive, productive and I-can-take-on-the-world-just-watch-me day.

Start your morning with a Gratitude List... and watch how your days begin to unfold more positively and profoundly as a result!

10

Mindfulness

*"Be happy in this moment.
This moment is your life!"*

In today's day and age, it's *so easy* to fill our days. Thanks to modern technology, everyone is *so* accessible. It's so hard to say no, when there's so much LIFE out there to say yes to!

Sure, it's good to be busy.

But being busy isn't always good for *us*.

And this is something that we, as women, particularly struggle with.

We're driven to do as much as we possibly can in a given period of time. We're natural-born multi-taskers. We are INCREDIBLY efficient!

We are **high-performers.**

And being a high-performer is a wonderful thing. But it can also be incredibly self-sabotaging. Because if you are a high-performer, chances are at least one of the several following statements apply to you:

- You experience extreme joy out of "getting sh*t" done and crossing tasks off your to-do list.
- You often receive praise or feedback in the realm of "I don't know how you manage it all" (and you love it!)
- You are a doer. Perhaps your biggest pet peeve is people who are all talk and no action.
- You have big goals for yourself.
- You hold yourself to very high standards, and become upset when things don't pan out the way you planned.

If any of the above sounds like you, then I say to you, "HELLO fellow high-performer!"

And while many of those above defining characteristics sounds like positive qualities (and they can be), they carry with them a heavy burden:

High performers often put the needs of others well-before their own.

Which manifests all too often in self-neglect at a deeper level. Maybe you're managing to keep the house clean, staying above water at work, and still getting in your regular four workouts per week, but are you fulfilled? Are you doing the things that make you happy? Do you even know what those things *are*? (Hopefully you do now, after our exercise on Day 8!)

I can remember so vividly when I first had this realization. I was, on paper, "crushing it," as the kids say these days. I was getting SO much done every day—between planning my wedding, holding down a full-time job, running 2 "side hustles" (including trying to grow Poised & Professional), pursuing professional performance gigs, and you know, being a HUMAN, I had a lot on my plate. I made lists. I crossed them off.

...And I yet was so unhappy.

I was stressed all the time, and even though I was being productive and balancing the crazy workload that had become my life, at a deeper level, something was missing. And it took me longer than you would think (and than I'd like to admit) to realize why: I wasn't spending time on the things that MATTERED. If you look at this list above, I didn't include: spending time with my family, making time for my relationship, keeping in touch with my friends, nurturing my relationship to God, appreciating all that I had... the really important things.

The first step to mindfulness is shifting focus what you "need" to do, to what you "want" to do.

There's a great quote from Eckhart Tolle that says, *"The power for creating a better future is contained in the present moment: You create a good future by creating a good present."*

Translated to high-performer language: Our tasks make up our days, our days make our lives.

...So, don't you want to make sure you're spending your life in a way that honors the things you really care about?

Of course you do.

But, like many things, it's easier said than done. And the best way to start is by being completely honest with yourself.

Do you like the way you're spending your days? Are you making time for the things that are really important to you?

If not—change it.

Remember, **you are responsible** for your own life. You don't have to go through the motions of a schedule that someone else created for you. You don't!

Be mindful of your time. It's the most precious resource you have.

Here is your Day 10 Challenge:

Depending on when you're receiving today's challenge, look back on your day, or look back on yesterday. What did you do? How did you spend your time? Was it mostly on things that—really—you didn't want to do? Were you running around, crossing items off a list? Doing this thing for that person, this thing for that OTHER person... and not much for you at all? If you're like most women, the answer to that question is probably "yes".

*Your challenge today is—the next time someone asks you to do something, **take at least 30 seconds and think carefully before responding**. Is this something you want to do? If not, say no. You're ALLOWED to say no when you'd rather not do something. Sometimes we need a reminder of that!*

11

Comparison

"Comparison is the thief of joy."
-Theodore Roosevelt

We've all heard that old saying about comparison: "The grass is always greener on the other side."

Well there's a simple solution to that.

If you spent less time looking over at your neighbors' green grass, and more time on fertilizing, cultivating, tending to your OWN grass... you'd find your grass to become a more beautiful shade of bright green than you could have ever imagined!

Right now, you're probably shaking your head thinking, *"It's not that easy, Alyssa!"*

Comparison is tricky for that reason—in today's digital age, we are literally FLOODED with images of what's going on around us. And, thanks to platforms such as Instagram, many of those images are beautiful, enhanced representations... that aren't always 100% truthful. Right? But they still make us feel as though we don't measure up.

As someone who works in the performance industry, I personally struggle with comparison almost every day. As an actor or performer, approximately 99.99% of your life is comparison. Auditions are, in essence, a panel of auditors who you may or may not know, comparing you to every other person they see that day. Comparison happens externally, and there's nothing you can do about it.

But comparison also happens *internally*. I can't tell you how many times I've sat in an audition or callback room, silently sizing up the people around me... It's just the nature of the game!

We must realize that **comparison leads to self-destruction, self-doubt, and most of all, unhappiness.** And as we've established that to be confident, you must also be happy. I've tried it without it, and it just doesn't work.

So how the heck do we fight comparison? How can we even start reducing it in our lives?

We can start by appreciating **what makes us unique.**

You can't ignore the things that make you different from everyone else—whether it's your heritage, your looks, your hobbies, or anything else—so you might as well **embrace them.**

Furthermore, embracing what makes you unique is a surefire way to stop comparison in its tracks. When you embrace your differences, you take yourself OUT of the plane of comparison—because the things that make you different, make you **incomparable.**

Another one of the most time-tested ways to combat comparison and coexist peacefully with yourself is by **living in the present—** something we talked a little bit about yesterday, on Day 10.

Another way is to make the active choice to focus on yourself—your strengths, your successes, your blessings... until you realize that no one else even COMPARES to all the awesomeness that you have going on.

But still that can be tough. Which is why we have today's challenge....

Here is your Day 11 Challenge:

*This is a tough one—today I'm challenging you to **take a total social media break.** Specifically, from Facebook and Instagram—if you have those channels, make the choice to NOT check them today.*

Start your day with your Gratitude List and your affirmations. Set your daily goals. And then don't let social media distract you from them. Just for 24 hours. You can do it!

And, most importantly, at the end of the day, be mindful of how you feel. Spend 5-10 minutes journaling about the day—what you achieved, things that made you happy, big successes... how do you feel?

12

Attraction

"We receive exactly what we expect to receive."
-John Holland

Today's #35DaysofConfidence focus is **attraction.**

No, not THAT kind of attraction... (although I guess it *could* be!) Let me explain...

If you've heard of the international phenomenon "The Secret," you're well aware of the **Law of Attraction.** For those of who were apparently been living under a rock and didn't buy into "The Secret" craze of 2006 (like me...), here's a one-sentence overview of the Law of Attraction:

Focus on what you want and you will attract it into your life.

If you focus on the things you like – the things you enjoy, the things that make you happy – you will attract more and more of them into your life.

It sounds simple. If you're like me, it sounds TOO simple.

But it works.

Because if you think about it, it makes a LOT of sense.

Here's an example: say you just bought a new car, and it's a white Toyota Camry. A fairly unsuspecting car, right? But after you buy that new car... you ALWAYS notice white Toyota Camrys! They're everywhere! How did you not see them all before?

This is because what is familiar to us, is recognizable. And concepts become familiar to us through **active awareness.**

What we choose to think about matters.

What we actively invite into our life will grow (whether it's positive or negative).

Jack Canfield, author of *The Success Principles* and well-known personal development guru, is a huge proponent of the Law of Attraction. According to Jack, "The Law of Attraction states that whatever you focus on, think about, read about, and talk about intensely, you're going to attract more of into your life."

This is what makes the Law of Attraction so powerful. By activating it in your own life, you will become a positive person who expects positive outcomes in your own life. Your expectations essentially become your own **self-fulfilling prophecies!**

So, what can we do with this concept? What can we do to make the Law of Attraction work for us?

We can make sure that the things that we think about, read about, talk about, DREAM about—are all things that we **truly desire!**

Resolve to replace hope with expectation.

Expect to achieve your goals.

Expect to be successful.

Expect to receive the things you want.

Expect to live the life you were meant to live!

We can actively control and manipulate our thoughts to be positive—to be constantly thinking about the things that we want. The most successful people in the world think and talk about what they want ALL the time.

And so should you!

There's no better way to end this chapter on the Law of Attraction than with a badass quote from a badass woman, Ms. Maya Angelou:

"Ask for what you want and be prepared to receive it."

AMEN!

Here is your Day 12 Challenge:

The Law of Attraction challenge is a great natural follow up to our Day 3 lesson on Realization.

On Day 3, we talked about the power of naming and claiming exactly what it is that you want in this world.

On Day 12, we're going to develop a habit to think and talk about those things... all of the time!

So, pull out your Aspiration Statement. Today your challenge is to **verbalize your Aspiration Statement out loud, before every meal or snack that you have.** *As we've mentioned before, the key to lasting change is habit-formation, and the key to habit-formation is* *finding a recurring time or pattern that you can rely on. You have to eat (and you do it multiple times a day...), so creating a pre-meal ritual is a great way to enact positive, lasting change.*

Think of it as a pre-meal prayer request... for yourself!

13

Negativity

"A negative mind will never give you a positive life."

Yesterday we talked about the Law of Attraction and the power of positive thinking.

But equally important and parallel to fostering positive thinking is *eliminating negative thoughts* from your life.

That's right, folks. In a week of learning dedicated to developing and maintaining a Positive Mental Attitude, we'd be remiss not to bring up negativity.

Negativity is a virus—once you let it seep into your life, it spreads and compounds easily. And it's all too easy to find yourself in a negativity spiral—think about one thing that's upsetting you, and another thought arises all too easily.

The good news about negativity though, is that it's 100% controllable. We are in charge of our outlook; we are in charge of whether our first response to a potential problem is optimistic or pessimistic.

According to Brian Tracy, another wonderful self-improvement thought leader, and my personal mentor, 95% of your emotions are determined by the way you talk to yourself as you go through your day. If you talk to yourself in a positive and constructive way, you will have an optimistic attitude. If you think about things that make you unhappy, lower your self-esteem, or cause you worry and social anxiety, you will have a pessimistic, negative attitude.

To be positive, you must deliberately replace negative thoughts and self-talk with positive thoughts.

For example, instead of dwelling on a physical flaw or something you wish you could change about yourself, make the choice to repeat to yourself throughout the day: "I like myself. I like the way I look. There is no one out there quite like me. I am special, and good things will happen to me."

Or, one I like to say all the time, even out loud: "Today is a great day."

The internal dialogue can be whatever you want it to be, it just has to be **positive.**

So, the next time you find yourself dwelling on negative thoughts— choose to replace the dialogue. Turn "I can't" into "Of course I can." Turn on your internal positive soundtrack!

Another great way to stop your internal negative self-talk is with the "friend test". Picture one of your dearest, closest friends. The next time you catch yourself thinking negatively about yourself, or doubting your own ability, ask yourself: "would I say this about my friend?"

As women, we have an unsurpassed ability to think the worst about ourselves. Worse than we would EVER think about those who are dear to us. We would never tell our best friend "Oh you're not good enough for that job," or "you're not pretty enough," or "you're not brave enough..." And if we wouldn't say those things to someone we love and care about, we certainly shouldn't be saying them to ourselves—the most important person of all! Remember, you are the leading lady of your own life—and leading ladies don't take crap from anyone (including themselves!)

Another way to cut off negativity before it manifests in your brain is to remove external sources. Negative people fuel negative thoughts. Identify the negative influences in your life and make a conscious choice to avoid them.

Let's close out this chapter on eliminating negativity with a quote from the ultimate bombshell herself, supermodel Gisele Bundchen:

"Having the strength to tune out negativity and remain focused on what I want gives me the will and confidence to achieve my goals."

Be like Gisele—tune out negativity and focus on the good!

Here is your Day 13 Challenge:

The key to eliminating negative thoughts is being able to pinpoint when they appear. Being able to identify what I like to call "negative thinking triggers".

Dr Daniel Amen talks a lot about the idea of ANTs, or "automatic negative thoughts" in his book, Change Your Brain Change Your Life. ANTs are one of the most harmful things for your brain and your self-esteem.

We are especially vulnerable in the morning, when we're still waking and shaping our mindset for the day ahead, so this is an ideal (and typical) time for ANTs to set in.

*One of the best things you can do to fight them off in your waking minutes **is refrain from checking your phone.** Yup, you heard me. When your alarm goes off, resist the urge to check your email, check your social media, check your texts—it's too much of a risk that you may read or click into something that causes you stress and anxiety... before you even get out of bed. And that's no way to start your day.*

Plus, think of all the time you'll save in your morning routine by cutting out the 5, 10, 15(?!) minutes of mindless scrolling-and-tapping.

*Instead, when you wake up, **say out loud to yourself, "Today is going to be a great day."** Repeat it as many times as you wish. Resolve to hold off social media and email checking until at least 1 hour after waking. By then you will have had time to do your repeat your "today is going to be a great day" affirmation, create your daily Gratitude List, and frame your mind for a positive day ahead.*

14

Selflessness

"Your greatness isn't what you have—
it's what you give."

———————————————

We're closing out Week 2 of #35DaysofConfidence with a curveball topic—which is why I love it so much and wanted to end our Positive Mental Attitude week with it.

Ready? Here we go:

To be self-confident, you must also be self-less.

...I know. It's tricky.

You're probably thinking, "If I think I'm awesome, shouldn't I be doing everything in my power to nurture and fuel my awesomeness? Why should I focus my time and energy on anyone other than my awesome self?"

Consider this: It takes a truly confident and self-assured person to be able to bestow a selfless compliment to another person.

Plus, giving a compliment **empowers** you. It **raises you up**. By giving a compliment (or better yet, making a habit of bestowing compliments regularly to those around you), you naturally become a person in a **position of positive power.** In short: it makes you a better person.

As the quote above says, your greatness isn't what you have, it's what you *give*.

You can better others on the journey to bettering yourself. And it will only elevate your own self-esteem and self-confidence as a result!

Here is your Day 14 Challenge:

One of my favorite challenges when I'm having an off week—or feeling generally crappy—is to make a goal of complimenting five people each day. This is what I want you to do today.

Compliment five people over the course of the day. They could be friends, family, work colleagues, or—even better—total strangers.

And once you do it for one day, can you do it for another day? Can you do it for a whole week? A whole month?!

Give away your goodness and see how it comes back to you in spades. Lifted spirit and increased positive attitude pretty much guaranteed with this one!

Week 3: Self-Improvement

Welcome to Week 3! This week, our focus is Self-Improvement.

And what role does "Self-Improvement" play on our road to confidence, exactly?

One of my favorite definitions of confidence goes a little something like this:

"A feeling of self-assurance arising from one's appreciation of one's own abilities or qualities"

If you notice, there's a theme to that statement—yourSELF, and your own abilities and qualities. No one else's. YOURS.

Up until this point in #35DaysofConfidence, we've talked a lot about vision and making ourselves better. We've thought hard about the things we want in this world, our dreams and goals and aspirations, and we've begun to train our brain to think positive, helpful, uplifting thoughts. We've started in the mind for a reason—because change happens
from the inside out.

But now we're READY to take our change up a notch, and focus on self-improvement practices.

The nature of the relationship self-improvement and confidence is cyclical. When you invest time in self-improvement—when you commit to becoming a better version of yourself, when you overcome challenges, define your values, invest time in your passions and your relationships—**you become more confident.**

As you become more confident, you are then empowered to take on *more* challenges. You are motivated to go after your goals, to push yourself, and to continue growing into a better, stronger, smarter person. You feel like a winner.

You feel unstoppable!

And this feeling is accessible to ANYone. All you have to do is start working on yourself. So, let's do that now!

15

Growth

"Are you better than yesterday?"

Over the next 7 days we'll be focusing all that falls under the "Self-Improvement" umbrella. And we're starting today with **growth**—specifically, how to start a habit of growth, become comfortable (or as comfortable as possible!) with change, and commit to it consistently.

And why growth? Well, as the saying goes, if you're not growing, you're standing still.

One of the best things you can do for yourself (and for everyone around you) is commit yourself to **lifetime of learning and growth.**

Richard Branson has this wonderful quote: "Every success story is a result of constant adaptation, revision and change."

But change isn't always easy. In fact, it *rarely* is.

But change is also necessary. It's inspiring! It Is the key ingredient in any success story.

Think back to the last "success story" you heard, the last nonfiction book you read, the last speech you heard. The most impactful stories never happen because the storyteller "kept doing the same old, same old". They happen because those people who inspire us *made changes to make their lives better.* They made the choice to take responsibility and ownership for the own life, and to DO something to improve themselves and their surroundings.

I've said it once, and I'll say it again—you are destined for too much greatness to be a passive participant in your own life.

And the first step towards change is **commitment.** So, let's do that now!

Here is your Day 15 Challenge:

*Make the decision right now to commit to positive growth for the next seven days. Look ahead at your calendar and block off **30 minutes each day** that you will spend investing in yourself and your growth. If you need to put it on your work calendar, do it now. If you need to set your alarm for 30 minutes earlier each day, do it now.*

Make the time for the work, and the work will happen.

16

Values

"When your values are clear to you,
making decisions becomes easier."
-Roy E. Disney

––––––––––––––––––––––––––––––––

As we've previously discussed, true confidence can only come from having a strong, sure sense of who you REALLY are.

A big component of what makes you YOU is **your values**. What do you believe in? What do you stand for? What virtues do you hold in the highest regard?

Unlike many other things, your values have a tendency to not change drastically throughout your life. Of course, there are exceptions, and life-changing events may in turn change your values, but for the most part—the things you believe in and the personal rules you abide by will stay relatively consistent throughout the course of your life.

And this is why values are so wonderful, especially when it comes to self-improvement and confidence.

Values play an integral role in the self-improvement process because they act as the compass that will help guide you down the path towards your best self. Especially in this crazy, chaotic, ever-changing world in which we live in, your values help ground you and keep you rooted in what makes you, **you.**

Staying true to your values and your beliefs has the simple, but profound effect of making you feel like your most authentic self. **Staying true to your values creates inner peace, which radiates out from you, like a warm beam of sunlight.**

When you have clarity on who and what you believe in, and you live your life in accordance with those values, you will feel confident, assured, and PROUD of you are. This is one of the many keys to true happiness and fulfillment.

But this can be hard to do if you've never spent the time to recognize what it is that you do and don't believe in. I think of the challenge of uncovering your values as a similar endeavor to the fun, flippant exercise we all went through at one point in our adolescent lives: dreaming up our perfect man/woman/significant other.

Surely, at one point in your life (don't leave me hanging here!) you rattled off a list that went something like: "tall, good sense of humor, loves animals, blue eyes..." And the list goes on.

And if it was so easy to list out the obvious traits we desire in a future spouse or significant other, it should be even easier to list out the traits we desire in ourselves—the things that are the MOST important to us in determining who and what we value.

So, let's take a crack at that in today's challenge, shall we?

Here is your Day 16 Challenge:

*Your challenge today is to spend 3-5 minutes writing out your **key values.** What qualities do you aspire to have?*

Make this list as long as you can—don't hold back!

When you finish, go back and circle 5 that are the most important to you. How do you want to be viewed and perceived by others in the world? What do you want your legacy to be?

From then on, the "challenge" becomes more of a consistent, active exercise in making choices that align with these values.

When you are presented with a choice, reflect back on your core values. Which decision will further you along the path towards those values? Which decision will lead you astray from those values?

*As Brian Tracy says, whenever you decide between alternatives, you invariably choose the alternative that **you value the most.***

Be conscious about your choices today, and your future self will thank you for it.

17

Character

"Who are you when no one else is watching?"

Legendary basketball coach, John Wooden, once said: "The true test of a man's character is what he does when no one is watching."

Although self-confidence has a lot to do with how others perceive you, and your ability to present yourself assuredly in front of others, TRUE self-confidence is being 100% okay with who you are when you're with no one but the most important person in the room: yourself.

The reality is: who you are when *no one* is watching is vastly more important than who you are when they are.

But this is hard to remember, especially in a technologically-centered, smartphone-loving world that glorifies ALWAYS sharing what we're up to! And not that I'm knocking it—hey, I love Instagram Stories as much as the next female millennial—but it does shift our perception of "reality" quite a bit.

As in… if I wear this outfit, but I don't post it/Snap it/share it on Instagram… does anyone really see it?

As in… if I go on this vacation, but I don't share a beautiful, wanderlust-inducing photo… will people know I went?

You get the picture (no pun intended). What I'm getting at is that it's **so** easy to become caught up in making sure that everyone is looking at us, that we lose sight of what's way, way more important: making sure we like the person we are when they *aren't*.

So, how do we address this? How do we make sure we're paying as much attention to the quality of our private life as we are to the judgment of our public life?

Well, mindfulness is a great place to start. (For a quick refresher on that, thumb back to Day 10). Spending time by yourself, *with* yourself (read: not distracted) is important. After all, no one's opinion of you is more important than *your own*.

And if you don't necessarily love the person you are when you're alone—without filters, without gifs, without any sort of editing? That's okay. After all, that's why you're here, isn't it? We all have things about ourselves we wish we could change. We all make mistakes, and look back on certain choices we made thinking, "Man, I wish I had done that differently." It's normal. It's HUMAN!

The important thing to latch onto here is the growth factor— making sure we *learn* from our mistakes. That we take time to process them, and reflect on what we can do differently next time to change and become better. That's pretty much the definition of character, wouldn't you agree?

I'm going to end this chapter with another John Wooden quote, because they're just so DARN good, and applicable to pretty much any aspect of life:

*"Be more concerned with your character than your reputation, because **your character is what you really are,** while your reputation is merely what others think you are."*

Stay focused on your character, not your reputation. After all, it's the only one of the two you can control!

Here is your Day 17 Challenge:

Sometimes the best place to start in improving your character and your feelings of self-worth is with a little bit of kindness.

*Today's challenge is simple, and maybe even one that you've done before: **complete a random act of kindness.** Pick up some trash off the street. Hold the door open for someone. Buy coffee for the person in line behind you... It doesn't have to be grand, and it certainly doesn't have to go noticed by anyone (in fact, that's kind of the point). It just has to be kind.*

18

Relationships

*"If you want to improve your life,
improve your relationships."*

While self-confidence is inherently a solo journey, it would be unwise to neglect the role of your relationships with those around you in developing true confidence.

Especially since we have already spent some time defining the connection between happiness and confidence, and relationships play a key role in our happiness levels.

A study from Harvard, which tracked 724 participants from varying walks of life over the course of 75 years, delivered significant findings on the "key" to long-term happiness and fulfillment.

The answer? Our relationships.

In a direct statement, Robert Waldinger, the director of the Harvard Study of Adult Development summarized: *"The clearest message that we get from this 75-year study is this: Good relationships keep us happier and healthier. Period."*

Said another way: The quality of our life — emotionally, physically, and mentally — is directly proportional to the quality of our relationships.

There's a reason why our relationships serve as primary sources of motivation in our lives. Relationships nourish and sustain us in our very core. They feed our souls and our deeper needs as human beings. From the very beginning, our relationships have a significant impact on who we become, and the relationships we prioritize continue to nurture and shape us over the course of our lives.

And yet, when we become busy, or stressed, or distracted, relationships are often one of the first things to suffer. (Remember in Chapter 10 when we talked about Mindfulness and the curse of high-performers?)

It's all too easy to become caught up in our lives and lose focus of the things that matter most, and the things, or rather, the people, who make us really, truly happy.

And the reason for this is straightforward (although still upsetting): although many things in life are deadline- and urgency-driven, *relationships almost never are.*

And so, we push that coffee date with our girlfriend, that phone call to our parents, or that quality time we've been promising our husband to "when we have time".

And let's be honest... who knows when that will be?

When it comes to your relationships—make a point to *make* the time. Investing in your relationships will not only show love and appreciation to the person you care about, it will nurture *your* soul too.

So, the next time you find yourself lacking energy, confidence or fulfillment, make an active choice to shift focus to your priority relationships, and you will find your happiness and self-confidence renewed and restored. Remember:

Improving the quality of your relationships will improve the quality of your life.

Here is your Day 18 Challenge:

Contact 5 people that you care about and **tell them that you love and appreciate them.** *That's all.*

19

Passion

"Choose to thrive, not just to survive."

Knowing what you are passionate about, what makes you feel good, and what inspires you, is a crucial step on the road to true self-confidence. The simplest way I can articulate today's lesson (without being incredibly morbid) is this:

Life is too short to NOT work on the things you're passionate about.

But what does that mean, "passionate"?

In recent years, I feel as though "passionate" has become an overused word, especially in the job interview space. "I'm passionate about marketing." "I'm passionate about copywriting." "I'm passionate about data analysis."

...Are you really passionate about data analysis?

Hey, maybe you are! And if that's your thing, the thing that truly makes you feel ALIVE, then good on you for finding it, and being able to work in it every day.

But if it's not, if you're spending the *majority* of your time doing things that don't feed your soul... then something needs to change.

Here's a little story for you. If you're not a fan of long-winded, dramatic personal anecdotes (I mean, who ISN'T?!), consider skipping ahead:

Once upon a time, there was a girl who loved to perform. Nothing gave her greater joy than being on stage, telling a story, and connecting with an audience.

Over the years, that girl grew up. Her time became limited and she was forced to make choices. The "right" choices. For her career, her future, and her stability.

She went to college and studied English Literature (since she had always loved writing, and was pretty darn good at it), which people scoffed at since it wasn't a "real degree".

So, she thought about picking up a second major. But what should it be?

Well she, of course, loved the theatre general education classes that she took, so she considered starting a musical theatre major.

When we presented the idea to her father over the phone one Sunday afternoon, he asked, "...But do you want to work in musical theatre?"

And the girl said no.

Because the question she heard was, "...But what will people think if you major in musical theatre? Where will that get you? Is that a traditional path to traditional 'success?'"

Instead she picked up a Public Relations major, because it seemed to have a little more established credibility in the working world, as far as "real" jobs go.

The girl continued to dance through college, but by the time she graduated, her performing days were done. She moved out West, got a "real job" working for a "big company," and started her "career".

And sure, she had fun. She was in her early 20s living in a new city after all, surrounded by opportunity, new friends, and beautiful beaches.

But something was missing.

So, she made more friends. And she changed jobs (a bunch of times)—hopping from this marketing job to that marketing job (how'd she end up in *marketing* anyways?) And she was successful. She made "good money." She had benefits and a normal schedule and a steady paycheck.

But something was still missing.

Then one day, five years later, she saw a notice for a theatre audition.

And for the first time, in SO many years... she was excited. She was on FIRE with anticipation.

So, she auditioned. And she got the part. And she performed. And it was *wonderful.*

She did it again. She started going back to dance classes. She found a vocal coach and attended acting workshops. She made connections in this new community, and found her way back to the stage, consistently.

And she found she was alive again.

Just a year later, that girl has **a greater sense of her purpose and understanding of who she IS than she ever has before.** She is living her most authentic life—the life she knows she was meant to live. She is happy.

Following her passions put everything in alignment for her, and helped her realize that all those marketing jobs weren't preparing her more the next, bigger marketing job, they were preparing her to use her passion of performance to spread confidence and fulfillment in the community of women around her.

And she has never been more excited to wake up in the morning, jump out of bed, and do the work she was meant to do, because it is 100% in line with her passions.

This girl, as I'm sure you realized from the first sentence of this little anecdote, is me.

And that's enough about me for today.

The point is—you DESERVE to follow your passions. You deserve to THRIVE, not just survive your own life.

Oprah said it best: *"Passion is energy. Feel the power that comes from focusing on what excites you."*

Find your passion, and do everything you can to fuel it. Your whole life will change in the process.

Here is your Day 19 Challenge:

Take a few minutes to answer the following questions:

- *What do you feel excited about?*
- *What do you love to do more than anything else in the world?*
- *What makes you feel ALIVE?*

Write down 3-5 activities that you genuinely love to do. *Do you love reading? Awesome! Is aerial yoga your favorite thing in the whole WORLD. Nice! Could you spend all day talking on the phone to people and feel 100% fulfilled? Good for you!*

"Normal" doesn't matter here. All that matters is that you write down 3-5 things that you genuinely, truly love to do.

Another quick note about passions: your passions can change over time. You, as a human, will grow, change and evolve for the rest of your life, so it's natural that the things your passionate about would change too! So, as you grow, make sure your change your habits to reflect your passions—don't become stuck in a rut of doing the same things because you "remember when you used to enjoy it". No. Life's too short! Remember: choose to thrive, not just survive.

20

Authority

"Commit to excellence. Every day."

Once you discover your passion and your strengths, it is your responsibility to hone your skills and become a true expert in your field.

It's not just your responsibility to the world—it's something you owe to yourself!

As we brought up before—you are unique. There's no one on this whole earth quite like you! Marie Forleo articulates this beautifully:

"You are here for a reason... No person has or ever will have the unique blend of talents and strengths and gifts and perspective that you have."

.... And it is your responsibility to USE that unique blend of talents, strengths, gifts and perspectives to discover your RFB and live the life you were meant to live.

And what the heck, you may be asking, is an **RFB?**

Your RFB is a handy-dandy little acronym I created. It stands for your **"reason for being"**. WHY do you exist? What is your purpose? How do you live the life you were meant to live?

Your RFB hits at an intersection of 3 different key points and understandings about yourself, many of which we have already touched on in this book, as well as another external factor that has to do with "making a living:"

- What are your **strengths**?
- What are your **values**?
- What do you **like to do**?
- What **does the world need** (Or: What can you be paid for?)

At the crossover of these 4 points, you'll find your RFB. And your RFB is completely, 100% unique to you. No one else will be able to make this same contribution to the world, with the same impact, experience and passion as you.

A side part to deciphering your RFB and your area of authority is to lessen time spent on activities that *aren't* your area of authority. After all, your time is your most valuable resource, and you need to spend it effectively.

But enough talking about RFBs in abstract. Let's figure out what yours is, shall we?

Here is your Day 20 Challenge:

Spend 10-15 minutes thinking through your answers to these 4 questions. You can download a free RFB worksheet (https://www.poisedandprofessional.com/RFB) to help you move one step closer towards figuring out your purpose.

If you're struggling, fall back on this wonderful quote from Bishop T.D. Jakes:

"If you can't figure out your purpose, figure out your passion. For your passion will lead you right into your purpose."

21

Learning

"Develop a love of learning."

―――――――――――――――――

One of the best things you can do for your confidence and growth over the course of your life is commit to a lifetime of learning.

For some people, this is easier than it is for others.

Personally, I have always been a huge nerd when it comes to traditional learning. I *loved* school and academia. Even today, I feel a sense of peace and excitement when I drive by or walk through a high school or college campus (weird, I know). In college, when we were prescribed a certain number of general education classes, I purposefully sought out random courses just because I wanted to learn about, say, German Culture and Civilization, or Art History. I mean, why wouldn't you want to take "Witches and Witchcraft from the Middle Ages to the Present" (which is a course that my alma mater ACTUALLY offers in undergraduate studies and that I am so jealous current students have the opportunity to take!)

Anyways, the point is that learning is important. Similarly to what we discussed about committing to a lifetime of growth and improvement, **the moment you stop learning, you stop growing.**

Especially after you have uncovered your RFB (using the exercise on Day 20), you will have received a huge gift from the universe in understanding what it is that you are passionate about, and how you can use that passion to contribute to the world around you. Most people struggle their whole lives to understand their purpose, so once you even begin to tap into what you think yours may be, you owe it to yourself to read more, grow more, and learn more about that topic.

But of course, you aren't confined to only learn about your topic of passion for the rest of your life. If something interests you, pursue it!

Rule of thumb: **If you're intrigued, explore.**

Plus, by exposing yourself to new schools of thought and information through reading books, listening to podcasts, browsing blogs and online publications, taking classes, or whatever other methodology best suits you, you are actively expanding your realm of knowledge and your understanding of the world around you. You become smarter, and you are equipped with more knowledge to be able to make better decisions about your future. And if that isn't self-improvement, and confidence-building at its very finest, then I don't know what is!

Here is your Day 21 Challenge:

Spend 15 minutes today reading something enriching, positive, and informative in your field of study. See how many days you can do this is a row!

Week 4: The Physical Body

As an actor, one of my favorite methodologies to study and practice is physicality—specifically, using the physical body to create and support portrayal of a character on stage.

The physical body can be incredibly powerful in relaying information, emotion and presence, both on stage, on screen, and in real life.

When it comes to self-confidence, everything we've discussed so far has had to do with developing confidence from the inside out, and improving our understanding of both ourselves and our practices to help embody our most confident selves.

It's true that confidence comes from within. When you are truly confident—when you have a firm understanding of who you are and what you want—it shines out of you, and radiates through every ounce of your being into the world around you.

However...

There are also a number of physical postures you can embody to strengthen (and sometimes even "fake") this aura of confidence.

We have all heard the saying, "fake it 'til you make it". There is a lot of truth in this statement, and many experts have devoted their life's work to understanding the relationship between body language and its effect on confidence and emotional response.

As I said in the Introduction, I'm not one of these experts. But over the years, I have seen and practiced a lot of manipulation of the physical body in the interest of exuding more confidence and poise. I have aggregated a bank of tactics that work and produce real results, both in external perception of confidence, as well as creating stronger feelings of internal confidence.

And I'm going to share those tactics with you right now.

22

Health

*"You're only one workout away
from a good mood."*

While confidence originates inside you, our physical body has a lot to do with how we present ourselves to the world. After all, it is the version of us that people actually see! And at the end of the day, the base factor that affects not only how your physical body looks, but also, and more importantly, how it performs and functions, is your **health and wellness.**

Like it or not—working out and taking care of your body is a necessary part of feeling (and looking) good.

There is a proven link between exercise and improved mood and self-esteem. Exercise is one of the most natural and reliable ways to improve your mental health: Regular exercise can help treat depression and anxiety, as well as provide natural stress relief, better sleep, and overall wellness.

Now, I'm not saying you need to be in fitness model shape, banish carbs from your life forever, or any of that nonsense (but if that's your jam, power to you!) What I'm saying is that, if you want to start feeling good, live a positive lifestyle, and feel confident, you need to start from the inside out, physically as well as mentally.

And if your body is healthy, it's easier for your mind to follow suit. In fact, research shows that specific types of exercise, such as strength training and yoga, increase our appreciation for our bodies, because they focus on the work you're doing, rather than the physical results. Which is what exercise and true healthiness is all about.

I can also say from experience that one of the best ways to start liking yourself and appreciating all that you and your body are capable of is treating yourself well. **It's a matter of respect.** If you disrespect your body by eating burritos, avoiding vegetables and not exercising, then it becomes pretty hard to be proud of who you are in general.

And if you're not proud of who you are—if you can't be your OWN advocate—how can you expect anyone else to advocate for you?

So, figure out what makes you feel good. And start there.

Here is your Day 22 Challenge:

Do something active for 20 minutes today. Go for a walk. Hit the gym and do some cardio or weight training. Take a Pilates class. Swim in the ocean. Dance around your bedroom in your underwear for 20 minutes. Whatever is available to you (and ideally, something you enjoy) will work—what matters is that you DO it. I can promise with 100% certainty that you'll feel great afterwards.

23

Overcoming Limitations

*"The comfort zone is the great enemy of
courage and confidence."*
-Brian Tracy

Today, we're talking about limitations. You know, the ones you
think you have?

The human body and the human mind are capable of incredible
things. With enough practice and preparation, anything is possible.
More often than not, it is our own self-limiting beliefs that hold us
back, rather than the actual capabilities of our mind and body.

We've all heard about self-limiting beliefs and how dangerous they
are. If you're new to the idea, in essence, self-limiting beliefs are
the negative, inhibiting things we think about ourselves. These are
thoughts that we just take to be true, maybe because we've been
told them over and over again, or perhaps because we've come up
with some reasoning in our own minds as to why they are facts.

But the reality is, most self-limiting beliefs are not facts at all.
Rather, they are lies we tell ourselves, usually as some sort of a
defense mechanism.

For example, let's say there's a job at your current company that you really, really want. It's your dream job! But instead of going for it, or doing the work you need to throw your hat in the ring and prepare for the interview, you tell yourself: "Oh I'm not qualified for that job. They're looking for someone with twice my experience." Because you believe this, you will never apply for the job. You will stay in your comfort zone, where you are protected by your self-limiting beliefs, and remain unchallenged, and, ultimately, unhappy.

Another example: Let's say there's a guy or gal you have a humongous crush on. But you're convinced that they'll never ask you out because: "Oh, he/she is way out of my league." Because you believe this, instead of making yourself physically and emotionally available to date this person—or, better yet, making the first move to ask THEM out—you stay single, unhappy, and comfortable in your singledom.

Do not read this as me knocking singledom, because I'm absolutely not. The point is, we tell ourselves the things that we think will keep us safe and comfortable. It's an act of **self-preservation.**

I once had the pleasure of listening to esteemed hypnotherapist, Marisa Peer, give a talk on how the brain works. As a hypnotherapist, one of the areas that she specializes in is helping patients overcome their own limiting beliefs by first identifying what they are, often through the use of hypnotherapy tactics, to unlock key realizations in the brain.

I listened to Marisa tell story after story of how certain patients' ailments and issues were not caused by physical issues, but rather by self-limiting beliefs and scenarios that they had created in their own mind.

One that stood out to me was a woman who Marisa worked with who—above all—HATED speaking in public. She was convinced that she was terrible at it, and that she hated it more than anything else in the world. And she said this all the time, even out loud to peers. She'd say, "Oh, I hate public speaking," and "I'd rather die than speak in public."

But low and behold, one day at work, she was assigned a high-profile presentation that she would have to give to many of her colleagues. And she stressed over it greatly, until the day before the presentation.

And what happened? She got very, very sick. And ended up not having to give the presentation.

You see, the brain is smarter than we give it credit for. If we tell ourselves (and others) that "we hate public speaking" and "we'd rather die than speak in public," then our brains will devise a way for us to NOT have to do those things. See? Self-preservation.

As we discussed early on Day 7, if you tell yourself something enough times (or if you are told something enough times), you will eventually believe it to be true. So, if you TELL yourself, "I'm not qualified for that job" or "that guy is out of my league" or "I could never quit my job and start my own business," then you won't do any of those things.

But if you force yourself to step outside of your comfort zone, change your internal dialogue, and break the cycle of self-limiting beliefs, then all of those things become very possible. It's all a matter of overcoming these limiting beliefs.

So, sometimes it helps to "shock" the system by trying something new. By proving to ourselves that we CAN do that thing that we thought we'd never be able to; by doing something that makes us think to ourselves, "I can't believe I just did that!"

And the physical body is a great tool for this. Which brings us nicely to today's challenge.

Here is your Day 23 Challenge:

*Break out of your comfort zone and **try something new today.** You become better by continually challenging yourself to grow, learn and do more.*

Take a new workout class, try a new hobby, cook a new dish… whatever it is, try something you've never tried before. If you need some inspiration, here's a list of 82 new things you can try today to build your confidence:

Activities for the Adventurer
1. Pack up a basket or bag and go on a picnic
2.Take a hike (literally)
3. Plan a day trip to a local landmark
4. Take a road trip with no end destination in mind
5. Visit a National Park
6. Go camping
7. Start a garden
8. Head to your local farmer's market and support local business
9. Watch the sun rise
10. Watch the sun set
11. Go star-gazing

Fitness and Health Activities
12. Dance it out! Take a Zumba class, or some other dance class
13. Embrace your inner ballerina and try a Barre class
14. Develop a "long and strong" body – take a Pilates class

15. Take a spin class

16. Go biking outdoors (rent one or use bike-sharing, if you don't have one of your own)

17. Lift some weights (it's a proven confidence booster with a host of other benefits!)

18. Try aerial yoga or aerial silks

19. Go indoor rock-climbing

20. Do a handstand or headstand

21. Meditate

22. Go for a swim

23. Try surfing

24. Go kayaking

25. Go stand-up paddle boarding

26. Go for a run

27. Go for a walk in the park

28. Sign up for a race

29. Jump rope (trust me, it's not as easy as when you used to do it on the playground)

30. Speaking of... go to a local playground and reconnect with your inner kid!

Activities for Animal Lovers

31. Ride a horse

32. Puppy-sit your friend's dog

33. Foster a dog (or cat!)

34. Go to your local shelter and adopt a pet (warning: this one's a big commitment!)

35, Volunteer at your local animal shelter

36. Adopt an animal through WWF's Symbolic Species Adoptions

Artsy Activities

37. Paint a picture

38. Paint your own pottery

39. Take a photography class

40. Draw or sketch from a photograph

41. Write a short story

42. Write a poem

43. Start writing your autobiography

44. Write a blog post (or, start a blog!)

45. Start a journal

46. Color in a coloring book

47. Listen to a new genre of music – find a playlist you'd never normally listen to on Spotify and give it a go!

48. Get cultured – visit a local museum or art gallery

49. Watch a classic movie on Netflix

50. Support live theatre – go see a show!

51. Go see a comedy show

52. Go see a ballet

Activities for "Going Back to School"

53. Look up the course directory at your local community college – see anything that interests you? Sign up!

54. Go to your local library and check out a book

55. Read a fiction book

56. Read a non-fiction book

57. Join a book club

58. Is there an activity or hobby you used to enjoy? Take a lesson!

59. Start learning a new language.

Activities that Feed Your Body and Soul

60. Try out a new restaurant

61. Look up a new recipe and get to cooking!

62. Host a dinner party! Inviting friends over for a meal feeds the body and the soul

63. Make a cake for absolutely no reason at all

64. Flex your ambidextrous muscles – brush your teeth with your non-dominant hand.

65. Research "feng shui" and apply it to one room of your home

66. Research "hygge" and apply it to one room of your home

67. Send a thank you note, or a "just because" note to someone you haven't talked with in a while

68. Take a bath

69. Get a massage

70. Get a facial (good skincare is a worthwhile investment, people!)

71. Give yourself a mani-pedi

72. Dye your hair a new color (or use temporary colors to go pink or blue for the day)

73. Compliment 5 people today

74. Pay for the coffee of the person behind you in line

75. If you normally drink coffee, drink tea for a day. (If you normally drink tea, drink coffee!)

76. Be the first person to say hello

77. Donate clothes and items you no longer use to charity

78. Volunteer your time somewhere that needs it

79. Turn off your phone for one hour

80. Don't complain for a full day

81. Don't say "sorry" for a full day

82. Book a plane trip to a place you've never been

Phew... if you can't find one thing on that list that you haven't done before, then you deserve an award. Try something new today—you may surprise yourself!

24

Posture

*"A strong confident person can rule the room
with knowledge, personal style, attitude
and great posture."*
-Cindy Ann Peterson

We would be remiss not to cover the topic of body language, specifically—your posture, in a book about looking and feeling more confident.

We all know the saying "you don't get a second chance at a first impression". More often than not, that "first impression" happens without any sort of verbal introduction. Your first impression to the large majority of the world happens from their perception of you, from your posture, body language, actions, and (last of all, actually) your speech.

What you "say" with your body carries a lot of volume!

Based on what I've read, body language and nonverbal communication conveys 80-90% of the weight when you're interacting with another person. So even if you're telling someone, "I'm so excited to be here," if your eyes are looking elsewhere, your feet are pointing in a different direction, and you happen to be crossing your arms... then your verbal message will not be received.

In addition, audiences *trust* nonverbal communication above your words and your speech content. Posture is the body's most honest indicator of our thoughts and feelings, so ensure you are sending open, positive signals.

Furthermore, even if you completely master the art of sounding confident, people will never believe what you say if your shoulders are slumped and your eyes are cast downward when you say it. As Allen Ruddock once famously said, "Your body communicates as well as your mouth. Don't contradict yourself."

Luckily, there are a few key posture adjustments you can make to project an aura of confidence, and even trick your brain into feeling self-assured. One of my favorite ones to talk about is inhabiting "high status positions".

As an actor, much of how performance is perceived by the audience is through the actor's physical portrayal of that character. In the instructional book, *A Body Prepares: A Complete Guide to Physical Warm Up Exercises for Performers*, Jake Urry, the author, introduces the idea of "archetypes" – which are conventions for actors to easily access specific physical, vocal and emotional states to portray a certain character. By exhibiting qualities of certain archetypes, purely on the physical level, the actor immediately is able to assume qualities that character would have.

For example, when an actor is portraying a warrior, he or she can inhabit common movements and behaviors that we as a society associate with this archetype, including a commanding tone of voice and moving with a sense of purpose and righteousness.

On the contrary, when an actor is portraying a crone-type of character, different physical behaviors can be used. The obvious choice is a to hunch your back and use a croaky-type voice (think *Wicked Witch of the West*).

The point of these archetypes is for actors to use them as a starting point in character development, with the key phrase being "starting point". Ideally, each character takes on a life of its own, that you create and refine into something unique.

The same can be said about confidence. There's no one-size-fits-all model for how to look and feel confidence. Instead, it's an act of personal development. But sometimes starting by practicing confidence behaviors can help to jump-start the discovery process.

So, to convey confidence in your own posture, make like a royal and focus on lifting your sternum, which instantly makes you look more confident. Your sternum is located in the middle of your chest and connects your upper ribs. An open, upright posture conveys confidence, authority, and high status.

Another tactic that you may have heard of if you have ever studied dance or practiced Pilates is the "zip-up" method: Starting at the area right below your belly button, imagine zipping up a form fitting jacket, all the way up to under your chin. Go through the motion and watch how your posture experiences a subtle, yet significant shift. This is a great exercise to use right before entering into a high-pressure scenario, such as an interview, a presentation, an audition, or even a first date, to instantly calm the body and project confidence.

Here is your Day 24 Challenge:

*The easiest way to start being aware of your posture, and to start addressing any confidence-undermining behaviors is to understand the idea of **open versus closed postures.***

A "closed posture" is any posture that makes you look smaller. Common examples are: crossing your arms, crossing your legs, hunching your shoulders, or leaning over and placing hands/elbows on a nearby desk or table.

An "open posture" is any posture that makes you look bigger—that helps you take up more space.

Positive, open posture makes you appear trustworthy, easy, confident—before you even open your mouth!

Your challenge today is to start being aware of your posturing throughout the day—when do you exhibit closed postures? When do you use open postures? Make a conscious effort to correct one consistent posture in your life. For example: "Any time I sit down in meetings, I will sit with my shoulders back, and head up."

25

Gestures

"What you 'say' with your hands, matters."

A specific element of body language that I really want to take the time to address here is gestures—specifically, how you use your hands when you are communicating with others.

There are countless how-to articles and videos out there about how to use your hands to get your point across, or deliver a better sales pitch, or connect with an audience. (Go ahead and do a quick Google search—I'll wait!) Being able to effectively use gesturing to drive home a point is truly an art form, and people want answers on how to master it.

But there's also a science to gesturing, and why it works. I recently watched a TED talk by Vanessa Van Edwards, interpersonal intelligence expert and public speaker, on this exact topic. Van Edwards and her team analyzed thousands of hours of TED talks, in effort to determine why some talks became "viral" and others were drastically less popular.

In their research, they found that the **least** popular TED Talkers used an average of "...272 hand gestures during the 18-minute talk, while the **most** popular TED Talkers used an average of 465 hand gestures." That's almost twice as many hand gestures in the same 18-minute time span!

So why does that matter? What role does gesturing play in likability anyways?

The answer has to do with our biology and survival instincts. When we see someone, the first place we look (or we *think* we look), is the eyes, mouth or face, but where we actually look is at their **hands.** This finding actually goes back to caveman days – when two cavemen approached each other, they looked to the other's hands first to make sure they weren't carrying some sort of weapon. In this case, hands are a representation of "friend" or "foe". Hands represent **intention.**

In addition, gesturing helps better explain verbal communication. In fact, Van Edwards' study concluded that using gestures can increase the value of our message by 60 percent!

And why is this, exactly? Well, there are many different types of learning styles that a person can gravitate towards. Most studies agree on seven primary learning styles: Some people are verbal learners, some are visual learners. Still others are physical, logical, social or solitary. I have even heard of "musical learners"—or people who learn best when information is conveyed through song and rhythm.

Most people are a mix of at least two of these learning styles. And if you're delivering any sort of message, it's in your best interest to maximize the number of learning styles that you appeal to. By implementing gestures in your delivery, you help to create a visual *and* physical depiction, to layer on top of the verbal communication that you're expressing.

Another key finding from her study? Similar to the overall power of body language compared to verbal language, it's also true that our brains give 12.5x more weight to hand gestures than the actual words that come out of a person's mouth.

In short, what you "say" with your hands, matters. So how can you improve the language of your hands? Awareness and self-study are a great place to start.

Here is your Day 25 Challenge:

In light of this revelation about the power of hand gestures, you challenge today is to tune into **how you use your hands to express yourself regularly.** *Are there specific gestures that you use multiple times throughout the day? Do you rarely use your hands at all?*

Here are some scenario-based questions to help you build awareness:

- *Where are your hands when you speak on the phone? Do you use them to gesture and articulate, even though the person on the other end of the phone obviously can't see?*
- *Where are your hands when you're talking in person with a friend?*
- *Where are your hands when you're talking in person with a colleague?*
- *Where are your hands when you're talking in person with your manager or something in a "position of power?"*

Being aware of HOW you use your hands to gesture on the regular can help you take steps towards better controlling them and using gesturing to help make you come across more confident and self-assured.

Once you have a handle on your current gesturing habits, you can start to work on specific, proven-to-be-effective hand gestures to help make you a better communicator and speaker. Van Edwards lists out a number of these, including listing, "listen up," and, my personal favorite, "I've got my shit together".

26

Smiling

"Most smiles are caused by another smile."
-Frank A. Clark

Another important aspect of body language when it comes to exuding confidence is what's on your face. No, not your makeup—your facial expression!

Just the act of smiling has a proven positive effect on your mood, and there are tons of studies and articles on this physiological phenomenon.

There's a wonderful, yet simple quote by a woman named Gitte Falkenberg: "Smile even if you don't feel like it. Your body language helps determine your state of mind."

And she's 100% correct. Success expert Jack Canfield elaborates on this in detail: "Putting on a smile, even if it's forced, can lead to almost an immediate flood of endorphins in your brain."

Endorphins are valuable because they, in addition to Dopamine, Serotonin, and Oxytocin, are the hormones responsible for feelings of happiness in the body. Therefore, endorphins released by smiling serve to improve your overall happiness and reduce stress. And smiling can give you an extra boost of endorphins when you need them the most.

Side note: Another natural source of endorphins in the body is exercise, which we talked about on Day 22. I mean, we all know the "Legally Blonde" quote; say it with me: "Exercise gives you endorphins. Endorphins make you happy. Happy people just don't shoot their husbands, they just don't."

This endorphin release you experience from smiling is actually triggered by the movement of the muscles in your face – meaning that smiling carries this benefit, even when your heart isn't really in it.

To make this reaction authentic though, the smile must reach the upper cheek muscles (those good old "crow's feet" muscles) and extend up to your eyes. And it's contagious – researchers at the University of Finland found that when they showed images of people who were authentically smiling and exhibiting real happiness to study participants, the participants themselves also experienced feelings of happiness and had a positive mood change. Conversely, when those same researchers showed images of people who were fake smiling to study participants, the participants caught no positive feelings.

This is to say that authentically smiling makes you more approachable. Say you go to an event (or an audition) that you are nervous or just less than excited about. This internal feeling will manifest on your face and actually make you less memorable... unless you do something about it!

Here is your Day 26 Challenge:

For today's challenge, I want to introduce you to my **"BSBS Formula,"** which combines lessons we've been talking about over the last three days on body language.

BSBS stands for: breathe, shoulders back, smile.

Three steps with a big impact. The appearance of confidence (and subsequent internalization of confidence) can be that simple!

Today, before you head into a meeting, start a new task, or even before you leave the house, take 5 seconds and try BSBS. It just takes 5 seconds, and it will be just enough of a moment of pause to allow a slight mood shift that will help you tackle ANY challenge!

27

Breathing

"Do not underestimate the healing power of breathing."

We touched a little bit on the power of breathing yesterday, and how it can help us to hit "reset" on our stress-levels, positive mindset, and confidence.

Breathing is something we *just do.* It comes naturally to us. It keeps us alive.

But we take it for granted, and we don't use it (I mean, REALLY use it) as often as we should.

In the busyness of our day to day lives, we forget to take the time to breathe. Which is unfortunate, since breath is the body's natural stress-reliever.

At a biological level, deep breathing is not only relaxing, it's also been scientifically proven to affect the heart, the brain, digestion, the immune system—and maybe even the expression of genes, according to a study published on NPR.

According to Mladen Golubic, a physician in the Cleveland Clinic's Center for Integrative Medicine, breathing can have a profound impact **on our physiology and our health.**

"You can influence asthma; you can influence chronic obstructive pulmonary disease; you can influence heart failure," Golubic says. "There are studies that show that people who practice breathing exercises and have those conditions—they benefit."

Furthermore, research has shown that breathing exercises can have immediate effects by altering the pH of the blood, or changing blood pressure. But more importantly, calming breathing exercises can be used as a method to train the body's reaction to stressful situations and dampen the production of harmful stress hormones.

So, to put it in perspective—integrating deep breathing and calming breath exercises into your daily routine can help soothe stress, improve your mood, and boost your confidence.

Here is your Day 27 Challenge:

*At the top of every hour today, close your eyes and do **5 "square breaths."***

Square breathing refers to a style of deep breathing where you inhale, hold, exhale, hold: 4 phases that mimic the 4 sides of a square. Square breathing is a simple, easy, and effective way to calm yourself and enjoy a few minutes of tranquility.

*So, **at the top of each hour today,** plant both feet firmly on the floor (either sitting or standing), close your eyes and complete 5 square breath cycles. Follow this breath count:*

Inhale 2 3 4
Hold 2 3 4

Exhale 2 3 4
Hold 2 3 4

...And repeat! Set a timer if you need to, to make sure you do it every hour. This exercise will help you soothe away tension during a stressful work day, refocus your attention, and re-energize you when you need it most.

28

Language

"Your words become your world."
-Nadeem Kazi

―――――――――

On the final day of Week 4: The Physical Body, we're talking about the **words you say,** and the power they have to influence your confidence levels, and how those around you perceive you.

I know we just spent a lot of time talking about how the words that come out of your mouth are often dwarfed by your body language, your posture, or your facial expression; but that shouldn't be interpreted as me saying that words are not important. Because they are. Especially when it comes to not what *other people* hear you say, but what *you* actively choose to articulate, and make your own reality.

The words you say (and the people you say them to) have immeasurable power to shape your progress and your potential. This is why we've placed such a focus so far in this book on affirmations, your Aspiration Statement, your power phrase, and so much more.

Simply put: **words have power.**

And yet, so often, we speak without thinking. We open our mouths before we turn on our brains!

Over the last few days, we've been talking about the weight of nonverbal communication. But if you nail your body language and posture, effectively use your hands to introduce yourself and set the stage for confidence... and then when you open your mouth you sound unpolished and unpracticed—it's all for naught.

The great thing about language is that it's so easily to control and improve.

And when I say language, I don't mean "using big words". I mean speaking with authority, confidence, and conciseness.

There's a saying I love, "Do not say in 10 words what can be said in 5."

As women, we easily gravitate towards the use of "filler words" – such as, "like", "um", "Does that make sense?", "sorry", and "just".

A great place to start on your journey to sounding more confident is by removing these seven words and phrases from your vocabulary:

Here are seven words and phrases to strike from your vocabulary right NOW to sound more confident and capable.

"Sorry"

This is not news – women have a tendency to overuse the word "sorry," especially in place of other words that we're actually intending to say, such as "excuse me" or "I have something I want to say." This video released a few years ago by beauty brand

Pantene does an excellent job of articulating the weakening power of overusing "sorry," and words that should be used in its place.

If it's absolutely necessary to use the word "sorry", swap in "I apologize," which sounds more deliberate and sophisticated.

"Just"

A.K.A. the four-letter credibility killer. What's the problem with "just?" Simply put, it devalues whatever words follow it. It minimizes the importance of your request, your question, your statement, and consequently– your overall impact.

Ellen Leanse, the founder of Karmahacks, published a post on LinkedIn about the overuse of this word in women's professional communication. Leanse explains her discovery of this phenomenon, and how it's underhandedly devaluing women's voices in the workplace:

"It hit me that there was something about the word I didn't like. It was a "permission" word, in a way — a warm-up to a request, an apology for interrupting, a shy knock on a door before asking "Can I get something I need from you?"

Leanse continues,

"I am all about respectful communication. Yet I began to notice that "just" wasn't about being polite: it was a subtle message of subordination, of deference. Sometimes it was self-effacing. Sometimes even duplicitous. As I started really listening, I realized that striking it from a phrase almost always clarified and strengthened the message."

A "subtle message of subordination" ... We use "just" to be polite, or not to impose on the person with whom we're speaking, because what we have to say is less important that what they're currently working on. That's the implication every time you use the word "just".

So, the next time you catch yourself starting off an email with "I'm just writing to ask..." or texting a friend "Just wondering what you think about..."

Revise your sentences. Revise your expectations. Revise your self-confidence.

"At least"

This one strikes a personal chord with me. A few years ago, I watched a brilliant TED Talk given by Dr Brené Brown on the difference between showing empathy and sympathy. (Brown is a research professor and the best-selling author of *Daring Greatly: How the Courage to be Vulnerable Transforms the Way We Live, Love, Parent and Lead*). In this talk, Brown explains how empathy fuels connection, but sympathy drives disconnection. Acting or responding empathetically means we try to take on the perspective of the person we're speaking with, and really recognize their perspective as their truth. It also means we refrain from judgment (which Lord knows can be hard!), and communicate in a way that respects their emotion and them that they are not alone.

Rarely, if ever does an empathic response begin with "at least..." Someone shares something with us that's hard to say, maybe even painful, and "at least" diminishes their contribution by trying to paint a silver lining around it.

As Brown articulates so pointedly: "Empathy is a choice, and it's a vulnerable choice, because in order to connect with others, we have to connect with something in ourselves that shares the same feeling they are experiencing. The truth is, rarely can a verbal response make something better. What makes something better is creating a connection."

Removing the phrase "at least" from your speaking vocabulary will help improve the quality of your genuine connections with others, and help bring you closer to them, rather than creating a wall (as innocent and unintentional as it may be) of disconnect.

"It's not fair"

Do I even need to elaborate on this one? Not to be harsh or anything but... life's not fair, people. Everyone knows this. And that's why this phrase is extra-harmful to your confidence and self-worth. Saying "it's not fair" suggests that you think life is supposed to be fair, which makes you look immature and naïve. It basically destroys your credibility.

Instead, stick to the facts, stay constructive and think positively. Instead of crying to yourself that "It's not fair that Chelsea got the part over me!" make the choice to act constructively. Did you do the best you could? Did you prepare thoroughly? Is there anyone you can ask for feedback on what went into the decision or how you could improve for next time? (Important Tip: It never hurts to ask! Really.) If you don't strive to learn from your experiences, you'll be sure to repeat them.

"This is probably a stupid question, but..."

First of all, you shouldn't believe that ANYTHING that comes out of your mouth is stupid. That's issue numero uno.

Issue number two would be all the negative self-talk that's sneakily wrapped into that phrase. To everyone else in the room, the question you are about to ask could be a perfectly normal question.

Or worse yet, it could be a question that they themselves have. So not only are you inadvertently calling yourself stupid for asking it, you're inferring that they are stupid as well!

Yikes.

These overly passive phrases instantly erode your credibility. Even if you follow these phrases with a great idea, they suggest that you lack confidence, which makes the people you're speaking to lose confidence in you. Don't be your own worst critic. If you're not confident in what you're saying, no one else will be either. And, if you really don't know something, say, "I don't have that information right now, but I'll find out and get right back to you."

"It's not my fault"

This phrase, and any other similar phrases signify one thing: lack of ownership. Ownership is indicative of confidence, control, and – most importantly – responsibility. If you utter the phrase "it's not my fault" (even if it's not your fault!), you're essentially saying, "I'm not responsible" – "I'm not an active participant in the outcome of my life." Furthermore, by removing yourself from the situation, you're subtly pointing the blame finger at someone else. And the moment you start pointing fingers at someone else, people will begin seeing you as someone lacks accountability for their actions, pride in the work, and general confidence in their abilities.

"I can't."

This one is the worst! Mostly because it's a lie. 99% percent of the time, when we utter the phrase, "I can't," what we're really saying is, "I won't". And guess what? People don't like hearing, "I won't" when they ask you do something. Saying "I can't" suggests that you're not willing to do what it takes to get the job done.

If you really can't do something because something out of your control is interfering, then you need to offer an alternative solution. For example, "No, I can't meet you to review that presentation today. But, how about tomorrow morning at 10:00 am?" Be specific in your alternative suggestion. A vague, open-ended alternative suggestion is just as bad as no suggestion at all.

But what's worse about the phrase "I can't" is the mental damage is does when you utter it. Just as positive affirmations can transform your thinking and abilities for the better, negative affirmations can wreck your confidence.

There's a reason actress Gina Rodrigues' 2015 Golden Globe acceptance speech for Best Actress in a TV Comedy made waves on social media – her powerful mantra, "I can and I will," struck a chord with the hearts and minds of viewers everywhere. Because, more often than not, the answer is "I can... And I will". And sometimes it's as simple as affirming that belief out loud to transform your outlook.

Here is your Day 28 Challenge:

*Reference the list of 7 words and phrases from this Chapter to remove from your vocabulary to sound more confident and **make a conscious effort to not say a SINGLE one of them today.***

Write them on a post-it note, stick it somewhere visible, and challenge yourself to make a conscious effort to avoid using them. If you're feeling particularly fiery, I suggest adding a "penance" element: if you say one of those words or phrases, then you have to donate $5 into one of your savings accounts (which is really a win...), or skip your morning Starbucks tomorrow. You can also set a reward for successfully NOT saying any of those words or phrases. Whatever motivates you—find it, and stick with it!

Week 5: Taking Action

"Vision without action is merely a dream. Action without vision just passes the time. Vision with action can change the world."—Joel A. Barker

3, 2, 1.... Action!

For the past four weeks we've examined and worked on our confidence from the inside out. We talked about self-discovery, re-framing your mindset for positivity, committing to self-improvement, and using the physical body to exude confidence.

And in our final week of #35DaysofConfidence, we're talking about **taking action.**

Why? Because at the end of the day, it's not enough to know yourself, be positive and grateful, have excellent self-awareness, improve your mindset, and hone your speech and body language maximum impact...

You must also take action!

Even if you were the most confident person in the world, would you spend your days hanging out in your house, wallowing in your own kickassery?

No you wouldn't!

You'd be out and about sharing your kickass self with the world and doing things that make you feel alive!

In this last section, we're going to focus on making everything that we've talked about for the last four weeks **stick.**

Heads up: This is going to be a highly interactive section, and I encourage you to use a dedicated notebook or journal if you haven't been using one up until this point in the book. These exercises are going to change your life.

So, let's get to work!

29

Planning

"If you fail to plan, you plan to fail."

On the first day of the last week of #35DaysofConfidence, we're talking about planning and preparing for success.

If you want to make things happen, you should *plan* for them to happen. As the quote above says, if you fail to make a plan, you can't expect for your goals to just magically manifest!

So, with that in mind, I'm going to make a bold statement here. Ready? Stay with me:

Anything you want to achieve is possible.

…You just have to have the right plan.

As we mentioned on Day 4, all success in life can be broken down into setting and achieving goals. And the connection between those two crucial actions of setting and then achieving is **planning.**

Planning is also essential for flawless (or even just successful) execution.

There's a famous saying most often attributed to Albert Einstein that goes: "If I had an hour to solve a problem, I'd spend 55 minutes thinking about the problem and 5 minutes thinking about solutions."

Suffice it to say that planning is important. Rarely, if ever, can something magnificent be achieved without an incredible amount of planning. Being able to successfully plan out your roadmap to goal achievement increases your chances of achieving that goal 100% (and you can quote me on that!)

And the great thing about planning is that it's logical process—it's a science really! The tough part is the creative brainstorming part (which for you, already happened back in Day 4, when you ideated your goals! Phew.) Planning is relatively easy—it just takes time and attention.

The first place to start when creating your Goal Achievement Roadmap is by identifying all the variables:

- What needs to happen for me to achieve this goal?
- What skills do I need to develop?
- Who do I need to work with?
- What can I control versus what can I not control?
- What are my opportunities?

Brainstorm every possible factor and stepping stone that will allow you to accomplish this goal. By getting your arms around all these elements, you'll be able to create a more accurate roadmap to goal achievement

Once you've identified all these elements, one of the best ways to create an action plan for your goals is by starting with a **timeline approach:** if you want to achieve this goal by the end of the year, what do you need to do each MONTH to achieve it? What about each WEEK?

For example, if your goal is to publish a book by the end of this year, it may seem a bit daunting at first glance. But let's break it down and quantify that goal. On average a non-fiction book should be about 125 pages in length. If there are 5 months left in the year, that means you need to write 25 pages a month, which comes out to less than 1 page a day. So, if you set a mini goal for yourself of writing just 1 page a day, you'll easily be able to achieve this macro goal of completing a 125-page book manuscript by the end of the year! It's all about having a plan.

Now not all goals are as math-friendly as this book writing example, but you can easily apply this strategy to pretty much any goal.

In some cases, you might not need a month or a year. A **sprint approach** might be better. With a sprint approach to goal achievement, you specify a set amount of time in which you're going to do EVERYTHING necessary to achieve your goal. Tim Ferriss, author of the *4-Hour Work Week* preaches about the effectiveness of goal sprints, and about the idea of simplicity.

According to Ferriss, before working towards any goal, ask yourself the simple question: "Am I making this harder than it needs to be?"

Often times the anticipation or overwhelm of how big our goals are cause us to become our own worst enemy in the planning process.

As is always the rule: **Keep it simple.** And find what works for you. Just make sure you DO the work of planning.

Planning is 90% of the work. You should always be planning your next step. Don't become complacent—when you stop planning, you stop achieving.

Here is your Day 29 Challenge:

Go back to your goals from Day 4—the 3 goals you set for yourself for the year.

*Select one of them—your biggest, scariest, most audacious goal—and create your **Goal Achievement Roadmap**, by mapping out every stepping stone on the path towards achieving that goal. Break your goals down into as many individual tasks and action items as you can. Pretty soon your scariest goal won't seem so scary at all!*

30

Achievement

"How do you eat an elephant? One bite at a time."
-My Mom

—————————

Making a plan is a great place to start. But change happens—*action* happens—through a series of small steps towards a larger goal. I call these steps "**micro-achievements**" where you achieve small wins, one after the other, for a long period of time, and then one day you can step back and say, "Wow, look at what I accomplished!"

My mom had this saying that she would repeat to me all the time growing up:

How do you eat an elephant? One bite at a time.

I know, it's a little weird (and unappetizing?), but don't read too much into the content. The sentiment is this: every big goal, every big plan, is scary. But there's always **some action** you can take to get started, no matter how small that action is.

I call this the **"Just Do One Thing" Method.**

The way the method words is this: when you're feeling overwhelmed by a task or a goal, think of one teeny, tiny thing that you can do advance you in the right direction.

More often than not, what you'll find is: after you "just do one thing", there's always a small step you can take after that... And then another step after that... and so on and so forth.

And the funny thing about this process is: the more small steps you take, the more empowered you become to continue along. These small wins or "micro-achievements" serve as confidence builders that inspire you to keep going.

So, taking that seemingly small action of just taking "one bite" at a time, can end up snowballing into an achieved goal way faster than you think!

When it comes to goal achievement, the name of the game is **momentum.** By doing one thing every day that will advance you in the direction of your goal, you'll be able to keep and gain momentum. That's why the "Just Do One Thing" Method is so brilliant. It's hard to NOT want to keep going after you "just do one thing".

So, when I'm feeling super overwhelmed, or unmotivated, I ask myself, "What can I 'at least' do?" What's one small thing (and it can be incredibly, incredibly small!) that I can tackle just to do *something.*

Sometimes that small thing is just talking about your goals. The most successful people in the world think and talk about their goals ALL of the time, because they have realized that goals are energizing sources of positivity in our lives. By thinking and talking about your goals, you'll be able to maintain positivity and momentum on the path towards achieving them. So sometimes, just talking about them is enough to motivate you to do *something*.

Remember: "Success is a series of small wins."

So, what can you "at least" do today to help move in the direction of your goals and ambitions? Let's figure it out.

Here is your Day 30 Challenge:

In the next few chapters we'll continue to talk about breaking down your action plan even further. Today, I want to challenge you to figure out something you can "at least do" today to advance you down your Goal Achievement Roadmap.

Let's use our previous example here and say that yesterday, when you laid out your Roadmap for your goal of writing a book, you listed one of your steps to writing that book as "come up with a list of five titles".

Now, that might seem to be a lot, especially if you don't have ANY ideas right now as to what you want this book to actually be about. So maybe you can't come up with five ideas right now. Maybe you're having an uncreative, uninspired day, and you're just not in the mood. (My first advice in this instance would be to turn to your Confidence Jumpstart Routine, but we'll discuss that concept in a few chapters.) If that doesn't work, then your challenge becomes this: just do one thing.

So, in this example, sure, maybe you can't come up with five titles right now, but can you come up with one title? Can you come up with one idea that you kind of like that you can build on? I bet you can! Give the "Just Do One Thing" method a try today, and make it a habit to "just do one thing" every day to advance you in the direction of your goals.

*So, your challenge today is this—**what "one thing" can you do today**? Develop a habit of doing "at least" one thing every day, and aim to make it in the morning, so it can set the tone for how you carry out the rest of your day.*

31

Urgency

*"Be unwilling to wait for anything,
especially your own success."*

Now that you've created your Goal Achievement Roadmap, and have mastered (look at you!) the "Just Do One Thing" Method, the next step is to add some urgency to your process.

Great success is dependent on urgency; specifically, a consistent sense of urgency. I can't tell you how many times I've created a brilliant master plan or new business idea, been super motivated to work on for about two weeks, and then had my excitement and workflow just slowly... taper... off.

Whoops.

But I know I'm not alone in this. New ideas are exciting! New goals are energizing! New goals build our confidence! And motivation runs high in the early stages of inception. The problem becomes *keeping* that motivation, and the subsequent work and action, consistent.

One of the best ways to improve your chances of remaining on track towards your goals and ambitions is developing a **steady sense of urgency** in everything that you do.

We know that building and keeping momentum is key to goal achievement, and urgency is the lynchpin to keeping momentum. But how can you develop a sense of urgency in your life? How can you make urgency something that (like confidence), "just happens" for you on a daily basis?

A great place to start is by setting aggressive, yet attainable deadlines for yourself. A deadline is the difference between "I'll do this someday" and "I'll do this by Sunday". Don't be afraid of deadlines. They are nothing more than a starting point. But the key to using deadlines successfully is... well, using them. Don't set flippant deadlines. This is a terrible habit to start, because once you start, it becomes very easy to continue delaying, and pushing back, and rescheduling until your deadline becomes irrelevant.

Commit to your deadlines as you would to a new business partnership—you wouldn't back out of a meeting with a client or prospective employer at the last minute, would you? Then why would you treat yourself and your own ambitions any differently?

If you're new to setting deadlines for yourself or if you've tried to set deadlines in the past unsuccessfully, raise the stakes to ensure success. Consider setting incentives for yourself. For example, if I complete this milestone by my originally set due date, I'll treat myself to that new sweater I've had my eye on. But ONLY if you hit the deadline! Incentive-setting is a great way to help you develop the habit of deadline achievement. It may be a shallow way to go after your goals, but it's temporary. After a while, you won't even need the incentives anymore, since your sense of gratification and the growing pile of accomplished work (with less and less to do) will motivate you to keep going!

Urgency can make all the difference in helping you create and live the life of your dreams. H. Jackson Brown, Jr, the author of inspirational book and New York Times Best-Seller, *Life's Little Instruction Book*, said it best:

"You must take action now that will move you towards your goals. Develop a sense of urgency in your life."

Be unwilling to wait for anything on your path towards goal achievement. Your future, highly successful self will thank you for it!

Here is your Day 31 Challenge:

Pull up your Goal Achievement Roadmap and **add a first round of deadlines** *to ALL action items. Be highly ambitious with these deadlines, but not unrealistic. A rule of thumb I follow: Give yourself at least one day more than you'll think you'll need to complete a task.*

There's nothing more demotivating that going into your Goal Achievement Roadmap and seeing an endless list of overdue tasks... Set yourself up for success with ambitious, but realistic deadlines, and start cranking on hitting them. I believe in you!

32

Control

*"Focus on what you can control,
and minimize the rest."*

As we've discussed throughout this book, preparation is a key to confidence.

In this chapter, I want to talk about the concept of **control,** and the role it should play in your preparation process.

I learned a long time ago—in high school, actually—the power of maximizing the impact of the things you can control, and minimizing the effect of the things you can't.

For example, I couldn't control what exact grade I was given on my chemistry test... but I could control how much I studied for it.

I couldn't control whether or not the teacher gave a pop-quiz... but I could control my attendance based-grade, and making sure I was there every day to maximize my chance of success.

I couldn't control any of the test-based impacts to my grade, but I could control making sure I always did my homework and turned it in on time.

The things I couldn't control were unknowns since they were ultimately determined by another person (in this case, the teacher). The things I could control were **100% up to me**. So, I focused on maximizing the impact of the elements I could control, and minimizing the impact of the elements I couldn't.

And the more I felt in control, the better I felt. The more positive I felt about my chances of success in the class, the better I actually performed.

This is referred to by experts as "The Law of Control". The Law of Control is a mental law (referred to by psychologists as the "locus of control" theory) that states that you feel good about yourself to the degree to which you feel you are in control of your own life. You are your happiest, most authentic, confident self when you feel that you are the master of your own destiny.

If you want to feel better about yourself—more confident, more motivated, more successful—then focus on the things you can control, and maximizing their role in your life.

Here is your Day 32 Challenge:

*Pull out your Goal Achievement Roadmap again. Go through the map and put a checkmark next to every single action item that's **100% within your control** to execute and achieve. Then, highlight ANY element that might require some external source outside of your control. For example, if your goal is to achieve some sort of certification or degree, then there's probably some sort of test that you need to pass. If your goal is to run a marathon, then you might not be able to control the weather on the day of your race. Highlight these uncontrollable line items to first become aware of them.*

Once you've highlighted these items, go through each one and write down specific steps you can take to prepare yourself for them. In the marathon example, although you won't be able to control the weather on the day of the race, you can control the location of the race (if you haven't yet signed up for it), your level of conditioning and training, and your attitude ("Even if it rains, I'm still going to have a great race!") You can also control your training conditions: if there's a likelihood it will rain the day of your race, then fit in some training run time in the rain!

The things you "can't" control become a lot more within your control with the right plan of attack.

33

Failure

"A setback is a setup for a comeback."

Right now, you might be thinking, "Um, why the heck is there a chapter on "Failure" in this supposedly uplifting and helpful self-improvement challenge book?"

The thing is, failure is actually a crucial element of success.

There are probably a zillion quotes out there on the role that failure plays on the road to success and achievement, but one of my favorites is one from the boss herself, Oprah Winfrey:

"Think like a queen. A queen if not afraid to fail. Failure is another stepping stone to greatness."

There's a stigma about failure that it's bad. If you fail, you lose. Right?

Wrong.

Because "failures" are not failures at all. They are **opportunities for learning.** As the saying goes, "You win or you learn. There is no fail."

And the sooner you embrace this, the better.

The moment you realize you can try and fail — and that everything will be okay — **then you are free to create, and become your most authentic, confident self.**

And when you're running headfirst in the direction of your goals and dreams, it's inevitable that along the way you will experience some sort of setback. But these setbacks, these "failures," are a gift, because they are opportunities for improvement and learning.

Yes, really.

Even the most debilitating failures are positive opportunities for growth. Mostly because the real reason they are so "debilitating" is due to our own pride and ego.

One of the best things you can do in your life to fuel your self-confidence and keep you moving in a positive direction of change, is to develop an **attitude of resilience.**

Ninety-nine percent of time, whether you worry about the outcome or not, everything will turn out okay. Worrying about failure and all the "what-ifs" that occupy way too much of your mental energy is draining. And pointless!

"Whether you worry or not, the world will keep turning. Life goes on."

But there is a way to stop worrying, and the fear of failure in its tracks, and use that time more productively. The way to stop worrying is to **embrace failure.** Whatever it is that you're worried is going to happen—whatever "failure" means to you—resolve to accept it, should it happen, and emotionally detach.

Most of the time, all of our stress and anxiety around the idea of failure stems from the "what if" spiral: going down a deep dark hole of all the bad things that could happen if we fail. But if you:

A) Define the "what if".
B) Resolve to accept it.
C) Emotionally detach.

...Then the stress and anxiety goes away. Failure becomes less scary, and you're able to see it for what it is (should it happen): an opportunity for learning.

Because when you're willing to stop at nothing in pursuit of your goals... you're already winning. But, let's take this intangible sermon and turn it into a tangible action exercise you can actually use. Shall we?

Here is your Day 33 Challenge:

*Take 5 minutes right now and think: whatever the goal is that you're working towards—**what would failure look like?** What's holding you back from diving headfirst into whatever it is that you're pursuing?*

Write it down.

A common answer is embarrassment. "If I fail, it's going to make me look bad/incompetent/stupid." Human beings are prideful creatures—we all are—but unfortunately pride can be a paralyzing emotion. This is an easier failure scenario to deal with, since the fear is almost all pride-based.

So what if you fail? Who cares? The only person who SHOULD care, is you. And your "failure" isn't a death sentence; it's a setback. It's a dead end that you just have to reverse out of and try something else instead. What's so scary about that?

And more so, if you "fail" and keep going, those around you will applaud you. They'll be impressed by your resilience, which will make it all the more impressive and gratifying when you do ultimately succeed (which you will!)

Or your answer may be more about your actual livelihood, like "If I fail, I will lose hundreds or thousands of dollars" or, "If I fail, I won't earn the promotion I've been working towards for years." That's a little harder to deal with, since it affects your income, or has repercussions on your family. But it's not impossible. **Nothing is impossible.**

Come up with a backup plan. So for example, if your worst-case failure scenario is that you would lose money, spend some time saving up, creating new income streams, and finding ways to earn more now. This can be as simple as selling some items around the house you no longer use, or something that ensures a little more security, like picking up (another) job. Or resolve to dip into your savings and be totally okay with that now. The more you can do to prep yourself for this "failure," should it happen, the less worried you'll be that it will.

The final step is to emotionally detach. Failure is not something to be ashamed of. Because it's not "failure" at all. And if you do fail, things will be okay. It's all a matter of retraining your brain to think about failure as an opportunity, not as a loss.

34

Proactivity

"Set yourself up for success in every possible way."

Throughout this book, we've talked a lot about the idea of responsibility, and the necessity of taking ownership for your mental state, your actions, and your reactions. I want to take this idea of responsibility a step further and really deep dive into how you can be a **proactive advocate** for your own success.

You can't always control what the world throws at you. But you CAN control how you react. And more importantly, you can control the position you put yourself in to be successful.

The best way to do this is to not just arm yourself with success habits, but to create a routine or series of routines for yourself where you can actively practice them in your life. We've gone through quite a few different success habits in this book so far, so in this chapter we're going to work on tying them all together in a way that works for you, by creating your **Confidence Jumpstart Routine.**

Many entrepreneurs and some of the world's most wealthy people credit routine as a crucial factor of their success. A consistent routine gives you the power to control your own destiny, and can help equip you to better deal with challenges that arise throughout the day with poise and ease.

A powerful routine can help you free up your conscious mental energy, become more efficient where it matters, become more creative, and continue to perform at your best, most confident level of output.

Now I'm not saying you need a routine that schedules your day out to the minute (although I'm going to bring that up shortly as an exercise). Instead I'm suggesting that you develop at least one routine that you can use to:

- Motivate and empower yourself to take action
- Bring about a positive attitude
- Calm nerves and anxiety prior to a potentially stressful situation
- Re-center after a long day
- Refocus on your priorities and goals
- Remove tension from the body

Among many other things! And this routine can be quick. In fact, I recommend only about 5 minutes for your **Confidence Jumpstart Routine.** Let's figure yours out now!

Here is your Day 34 Challenge:

*I want to challenge you to create your personal **Confidence Jumpstart Routine** using some of the elements we've discussed and exercises we've completed over the last 34 days.*

Aim to create a 5-minute routine that you can use to "reset" your confidence and motivation levels. Choose from the list of activities below and select 5 to compose your own Confidence Jumpstart

Routine (one activity per minute). Mix and match your chosen 5 exercises in a way that makes sense to you, and that you can consistently rely on and turn to as a routine to help you refocus and jumpstart your confidence.

1. *Write down 10 things that make you unique (Day 2: Identity)—This will reaffirm some of the qualities you like about yourself, and remind you that you are truly special.*

2. *Repeat your Aspiration Statement out loud, or write it down (Day 3: Realization)—This will remind you of you of your ultimate goal: the life you want to create for yourself.*

3. *Rewrite your goals (Day 4: Goal-Setting)—Remind yourself of your goals and your power to achieve them.*

4. *Repeat out loud to yourself "I am responsible" (Day 5: Responsibility)—Reframe your mindset for taking action and empowering yourself.*

5. *Do one of your strength activities (Day 6: Motivation)—Do one of the activities that you know makes you feel stronger.*

6. *Repeat your three-word power phrase out loud (Day 7: Mindset)—Remind yourself of the attributes you most admire and want to strengthen in yourself.*

7. *Do one of the things that you know makes you happy (Day 8: Happiness)—Happiness creates confidence!*

8. *Write a Gratitude List (Day 9: Gratitude)—Write down everything you are grateful for at this moment in time to remind yourself of all the good things in your life.*

9. Practice your posture with the "zip up method," or hold open "power poses" for one minute (Day 24: Posture)—Reinforce confident behavior through your body's actions.

10. Practice square breathing for one minute (Day 27: Breath)—Calm your nerves and refocus your mind by bringing attention to your breath.

BONUS! More Proactivity-Focused Exercises:

Here are a few MORE exercises I've found to work well for setting yourself up for success, and creating the kind of life where you can be your most confident, happy, fulfilled self.

Craft Your Ideal Day: This is a fun one. Take 30 minutes to sit down and plan out your ideal day in hourly increments. This exercise hearkens back to Steve Jobs' famous daily question, "If today was the last day of my life would I want to do what I'm about to do today?"

Having a sense of how you'd spend your day if it were entirely up to you, reinforces the things you care about (and the things you don't). Once you have a sense of what your ideal day would look like, work on making it a reality.

The Proactive To-Do List: Many of us have been trained to write out our daily to-do list each morning to set our goals and intentions for the day. However, waiting until the morning-of to make your to-do list can actually set you up for failure, as it makes you highly reactive to any requests, communication, and social media posts you've already seen by the time you make your list.

Instead, try making a "Proactive To-Do List" and writing out your key action items for the next day the night before. This puts you in total control of your time for the next day, which will in turn affect *your mindset positively. Remember: Respect your own time: it is your most valuable resource!*

35

Courage

"The best time to jump is right before you're ready."

The best and most natural way I can think to end this book is with a chapter on Courage.

Because being confident takes courage. Changing your daily habits to become your best self, and challenging yourself to step outside your comfort zone takes courage. Just the act of getting started takes courage.

Everything seems overwhelming until you start. You can plan and set deadlines and practice your affirmations, but at the end of the day, **you need to start.**

And, as the quote at the beginning of this chapter says, best time to jump is *right before* you're ready.

Because you'll never be "ready". Not really. There's always one more thing you could do to be more prepared, one more exercise you can complete, one more thing you can learn... but sometimes you need to just start.

Sometimes, you need to just go ahead and raise your hand in the classroom.

Sometimes, you need to just speak up in the meeting.

Sometimes, you need to say, out loud, when you think you have a better idea.

Sometimes you just need to ask that guy out.

Whatever it is, the most courageous thing you can do is to *just do it.*

And if it makes you feel a little bit uncomfortable, great! It should. Growth happens when you step outside of your comfort zone. You become a better, stronger person when you step outside your comfort zone.

Beginning your journey to confidence and authentic living is one of the most courageous acts you can take.

It's only after you start, and take this crucial step outside of the familiar comfort zone that you can embark on the path towards discovering your true potential, and begin living your best, most confident, most authentic life.

And once you do, you'll find that you are unstoppable!

Here is your Day 35 Challenge:

*Getting started is exciting, but continuing on can be more of a struggle. To help you stay accountable towards your goals, **identify your personal support group**: a group of 3-5 people who you are going to tell about your goals, and more importantly, your deadlines.*

Choose your personal support group carefully. Choose people who you look up to and you know will encourage you. Choose people who have the courage to make confident life decisions that inspire you to do the same. Bravery inspires bravery. Surround yourself with people who inspire you to be better—who inspire you to be the absolutely best version of yourself—and your success will be inevitable.

And as you find success and fulfillment in life, be aware that you are inspiring others to do the same. Positive energy and confidence are infectious, and once you begin living your most authentic, confident life, don't be surprised when the people around you are inspired (by you!) to do the same.

Conclusion

"I was always looking outside myself for strength and confidence, but it comes from within. It is there all the time."
-Anna Freud

If there's one thing that I want you to take away from this book and these exercises it's this:

You are not a passive participant in your own life.

Life is not something that just happens to you. You are responsible for taking ownership of your life, and how you spend your time. If you don't like something, change it.

Period.

Those people who you have always looked up to: who life seems to happen effortlessly for, who have "all the luck"? That's not by chance. Those people have taken their life into their own hands— they are playing a starring role in their own lives.

And so can you.

There's only 1% of people out there living their dreams. You can be a part of that 1%!

For many of you, that means that some real change needs to happen over the next month/couple of months/year/years.

Trust your gut, rely on your training and your practices, and make it happen. You can do this!

I am a firm believer in the power of purpose. Once you find that thing that you are meant to do this world, and you pursue it passionately and with intention, you will discover an authentic and meaningful quality of life where everything seems to fall into place. Once you begin pursuing your purpose, the universe will conspire to continue to help make good things happen for you. Good breeds more good. And those "lucky people" you've always admired? Soon you'll find that you're one of them.

You deserve to live the life you've always imagined for yourself. So go out there and make it happen!

If you're ready to take the next step on YOUR journey to true confidence and authentic living, access my free video training session at poisedandprofessional.com/free-training

About the Author

For as long as she can remember, Alyssa has been fascinated by the science of what makes people confident, effective communicators. This helped to inspire her love for theatre and the performing arts at a young age.

Alyssa studied communications at Penn State University, where she danced competitively as a member of the national championship-winning Penn State Lionettes Dance Team. After college, Alyssa worked in corporate marketing for 8 years where she learned the power of effective confidence and communication tactics to advance and thrive in the workplace.

Today, her mission is to **equip and empower confident female creators to success**.

She now lives and works in San Diego as an actor, and teaches women of all ages the power of developing confidence through her blog and coaching site, *PoisedandProfessional.com*.

Alyssa lives with her husband, Mike, and their extremely photogenic Bernese Mountain Dog, Georgie.

Resources

Chapter 4:

https://www.linkedin.com/pulse/only-three-percent-population-set-goals-objectives-john-kapeleris

Chapter 6:

https://en.wikipedia.org/wiki/Jim_Ryun
http://www.businessinsider.com/jim-rohn-youre-the-average-of-the-five-people-you-spend-the-most-time-with-2012-7

Chapter 10:

https://www.poisedandprofessional.com/

Chapter 12:

http://jackcanfield.com/blog/put-the-action-in-attraction/

Chapter 13:

https://www.briantracy.com/blog/personal-success/be-the-best-you-7-keys-to-a-positive-personality/
https://www.amazon.com/Change-Your-Brain-Revised-Expanded/dp/110190464X

Chapter 16:

https://www.briantracy.com/blog/sales-success/clarify-your-values/

Chapter 18:

http://www.adultdevelopmentstudy.org/grantandglueckstudy

Chapter 20:

https://s3.amazonaws.com/marieforleo.com/MarieForleoHowTo
GetAnythingYouWant.mp3
https://www.poisedandprofessional.com/RFB

Chapter 22:

https://www.helpguide.org/articles/healthy-living/the-mental-health-benefits-of-exercise.htm

Chapter 23:

https://www.marisapeer.com/

Chapter 24:

https://www.psychologytoday.com/us/blog/beyond-words/201109/is-nonverbal-communication-numbers-game

Chapter 25:

https://www.youtube.com/watch?v=cef35Fk7YD8
https://www.learning-styles-online.com/overview/
https://www.scienceofpeople.com/hand-gestures/

Chapter 26:

http://jackcanfield.com/blog/cheer-up-fast/

Chapter 27:

https://www.npr.org/2010/12/06/131734718/just-breathe-body-has-a-built-in-stress-reliever
http://www.sweetescapeyoga.com/simple-stress-relief-wsquare-breathing/

Chapter 28:

https://www.youtube.com/watch?v=TcGKxLJ4ZGI
https://www.linkedin.com/pulse/just-say-ellen-petry-leanse/
https://www.youtube.com/watch?v=1Evwgu369Jw

https://www.theladders.com/career-advice/ten-things-smart-people-never-say
https://www.youtube.com/watch?v=veftkYtLVBM

Chapter 29:

http://writenonfictionnow.com/how-long-should-a-manuscript-be/
https://tim.blog/

Will You Review Me?

Thank you for reading my book! I really appreciate all your feedback and I love hearing what you have to say.

I need your input to make the next version of this book and my future books better.

Please leave me an honest review on Amazon, letting me know what you thought of the book.

Thanks so much! I appreciate you.

Alyssa A. Austin

Made in the USA
Columbia, SC
04 February 2019